The
# EFFICIENT VEGAN

# The
# EFFICIENT VEGAN

## WHOLE FOOD RECIPES THAT WILL CHANGE YOUR
## PERCEPTION OF THE PLANT-BASED LIFESTYLE

### Nicole Gumpel and Paige Mayfield

PHOTOGRAPHS BY KRISTY WOOD

Two Girls in Black, LLC
New York, NY

Library of Congress Control Number:
2013942967

ISBN 978-0-615-81364-6
Printed in the USA


Styling and Design by Kristy Wood and The Efficient Vegan
Photographs by Kristy Wood
(photographs on pages 6, 8, and back cover
by Eric Martinez)
Symbols: bioraven/shutterstock

The Efficient Vegan is intended soley for informational purposes and is not
intended to constitute, or should not be considered in any way medical
advice. The Efficient Vegan should not serve as a substitue for the advice
of a qualified medical physician or other qualified health care provider.

Two Girls In Black, LLC
www.theefficientvegan.com

# ACKNOWLEDGMENTS

There would be no *The Efficient Vegan* without the multifaceted contributions from some amazing people.

Thank you, Kristy Wood. There isn't room to thank you for all the ways that you helped. Above all, you made our food beautiful.

Thank you also to our parents, Sharon and Joel Gumpel and Linda and Tom Mayfield, who have supported us our entire lives, and especially in this project. And to our siblings Warren and Molly for being soundboards, proofreaders, and cheerleaders.

We are also incredibly grateful to our friends, Peg, Jacquie, TTTodd, Candice, Nadav, Krystal, Paris and David, Erica and Ivory, Mewi, Jason, Gilwit, Little Evil, Eric M., PP, Jaime McD, Ian, Jess, Coop, Libby, MP, and Phillip. You all went out of your way to support this project and we cannot thank you enough.

And, of course, thank you to all of our kickstarter backers. Your foresight and trust in our vision provided us with the financing that we needed to create the product that we always imagined.

We love you.

"Sausage" Kale Pizza (page 160)

**PAIGE**

I can't lie. Vanity was my primary motivation for adopting a vegan diet. After I graduated from college it occurred to me that I wasn't going to be young forever. I realized that I had to make some lifestyle changes to maintain my youth, so I began feverishly researching diet and exercise. I've always been on the "hippie" side, so I gravitated toward holistic nutritional guides. After reading about different vegan diets and how they preserve skin and hair quality while also keeping you thin, I was sold.

I am an extremist. So within a month of deciding to make the change, I was a full-on raw-foodist, only eating uncooked fruits, vegetables, sprouted grains, nuts, and seeds. It wasn't easy adopting this diet twelve years ago in North Carolina. The mere mention of health food got you a cross look, at best, and the few health food stores around me had no idea what a raw-foodist was. Out of determination and necessity, I learned how to prepare my own food and how to fit this increased participation in food preparation into my lifestyle.

The changes in my health and appearance were more drastic than I could ever have imagined. I immediately lost weight and improved my muscle tone. My hair began to grow faster and my skin almost glowed. I have not been sick since, nor used any topical or internal medications; it's been over ten years.

While my experience was less gradual than most, I still understand and resonate with the progression to a totally vegan lifestyle. I was immediately immersed in the dietary changes, but it took years before the lifestyle implications of being a vegan clicked. I have always loved animals, but like most people, had never really considered their sacrifice in much of what we wear and consume. Human beings make it convenient like that. We don't have to look a cow in the face, choose our convenience over its life, and then kill it ourselves and use its skin.

We can just walk into a store and buy a leather coat.

When I lost my dog, Fang, it finally clicked that the ethical reasons for being a vegan superseded the health benefits. I began to notice how we make it convenient to use products we wouldn't otherwise be comfortable using if we were aware of who was being harmed as a result. Once I eliminated all animal products from my life, everything came together and made more sense.

Realizing this was like finding your closest life-long friend.

Which, coincidentally, I had. When I met Nikki in 2007, I knew I'd found a kindred spirit. She immediately "got it." I had found my partner in crime.

## NIKKI

At first I thought Paige was nuts. We both started working at Barneys, New York at the same time and were the same age. Naturally we started chatting during the down times. I couldn't believe it. I mean, I've never been a huge meat eater; but NO chicken? Cheese? Fish? I honestly couldn't believe what she was saying! But I was intrigued. After a couple of weeks, we started hanging outside of work and I noticed her energy levels. We would stay out most of the night and she would come to work totally fine, while I had a massive hangover. That definitely got my attention and I decided to start making some changes.

Looking back, becoming vegan came pretty naturally to me, too. I began cutting back on animal products and I started feeling and looking better. People started noticing and asking about what I'd been doing. I was able to stay out later and come to work more refreshed. I felt great and didn't even miss any of the foods that I'd given up.

Let's be honest… I loved my 25-year-old lifestyle and I've been able to sustain it all these years by eating a plant-based diet. I'm no homebody; and despite drinking and staying out late most nights, I look and feel younger than ever. Eating a nutrient-rich, well-balanced, and vegan diet is truly the fountain of youth!

## NIKKI AND PAIGE

So there we were: out every night, yet totally capable every morning. No one around us could believe that we had so much energy. Paige had left Barneys and opened a raw-vegan juice bar where we spent most of our time. We had no idea it would change our lives forever. We were having the time of our lives and at the same time, really helping people. We were introducing vegan foods to an entirely new demographic. Everyone was into it and noticed the benefits immediately.

We had a good run and when we closed, the customers were beyond disappointed. They loved the lifestyle but weren't confident enough to do it on their own.

After the juice bar, we designed a revolving vegan menu for a meal delivery service. It was a challenge at first. We wanted to keep our costs low, but we weren't willing to sacrifice the quality of the food. We also weren't serving up bland tofu dinners! All of the ingredients had to be fresh, organic, and whole. And the meals had to taste good! We modeled our recipes each week after conventionally appealing meal ideas and eliminated waste by using overlapping ingredients. We were creating amazing food that even non-vegans loved while staying within our budget. We knew we had a good thing going.

We started cataloging our recipes and ideas on efficiency and developed a code system. Through backward reasoning we found ways for anyone to incorporate this healthy and homemade food into their diet. And here it is! *The Efficient Vegan*; organic and plant-based recipes that will change the way you perceive vegan foods!

We want to show you that it is possible to lead a very healthy and vegan lifestyle without missing out on anything; and without wearing tie-dyes and beating bongos.  A better you is easier and more economical than you think. And we want to help you learn how to integrate these life-changing foods into your life!

# Why VEGAN?

> *"Nothing will benefit human health or increase chances for survival of life on Earth as much as the evolution of the vegetarian diet"*
> *-Albert Einstein, German Physicist[1]*

To us, the answer to this question is incredibly obvious. There is no downside to the plant-based lifestyle: it's good for your health, makes you look and feel better, and is obviously more sensitive to animals and to the environment. And contrary to conventional perceptions, it is delicious. But what exactly does it mean to be a vegan?

This is the more complicated question. There are many different interpretations of this lifestyle and, of course, countless labels. To explain veganism in the simplest way, we will define the three types of "vegans" as we see it:

## LIFESTYLE VEGANS

## DIETARY VEGANS

## RAW VEGANS

Keep in mind, the definition of what it is to be a vegan is somewhat controversial and these are labels that we use to better explain the lifestyle. We will also overview what we feel are the main benefits for choosing a vegan lifestyle:

## PERSONAL HEALTH

## ANIMAL RIGHTS

## ENVIRONMENTAL PROTECTION

Don't be intimidated by the definitions or feel like any less of a participant for not living up to any vegan's expectations. There is no such thing as a perfect vegan. And in today's society, even those who are extremely strict occasionally break the rules.

Let's start at the beginning....

## VEGAN ORIGINS

The term vegan was conceived by Donald Watson, a member of The Vegetarian Society of England. He and a group of other concerned members left to start a new society of vegetarians who sought to lead a totally plant-based lifestyle free from all animal products, including dairy, eggs, and honey. He coined the term vegan by taking the first three and last two letters of the word vegetarian, because vegan "starts with vegetarianism and carries it through to its logical conclusion."[2] The Vegan Society, established in 1944, also encouraged the manufacture and consumption of clothing and shoes that were produced without animal products. From its origins, veganism was intended to be a full lifestyle, not just a diet.[3]

The American Vegan Society was formed in 1960 and more completely defined the boundaries of veganism using the acronym for the Sanskrit word AHIMSA, meaning "nonharming or noninjuring."[4]

**A**bstinence from animal products
**H**armlessness with reverence for life
**I**ntegrity of thought word and deed
**M**astery over oneself
**S**ervice to humanity
**A**dvancement of understanding and truth[5]

**A VEGAN DIET** is one totally free of animal products and any additives derived from animals. This includes animal flesh, dairy products, animal eggs, and honey.

**A VEGAN LIFESTYLE** is free from all animal products and any product or service that involved or involves the exploitation of animals. This includes the consumption of products made from leather, fur, wool, silk, and feathers; and any products that were derived using vivisection (animal testing). This also includes participation in activities that exploit animals including circuses, animal races, horseback riding, and zoos.

# LIFESTYLE VEGANS

Based on the origins of veganism, we have defined a Lifestyle Vegan as one who follows the six aforementioned pillars of veganism (ASHIMA) and who considers the respect for and aid to all life at all times. A Lifestyle Vegan not only eats a vegan diet and completely avoids all animal products and their byproducts, but is also devoted to the protection of all life through selfless activism.[6] Because veganism was developed as a lifestyle and not just a diet, Lifestyle Vegans consider themselves the only true vegans, and all others vegetarians.[7]

# DIETARY VEGANS

Dietary Vegans have chosen to eliminate animal products, including dairy and eggs, from their diet only. Whether it's because they haven't yet made the connection to the lifestyle implications or because their decision to become vegan is solely based on the health benefits, they continue to consume products and merchandise that contain animal products. Dietary Vegans may wear leather, silk, and wool, and use products tested on animals.

# RAW FOOD VEGANS

Raw Food Vegans can be either Dietary or Lifestyle Vegans, but only eat vegan food that has never been exposed to temperatures over 110 degrees Fahrenheit. Based on the theories of Edward Howell, Raw Food Vegans subscribe to the belief that the body has a finite ability to produce enzymes and if not supplemented with enzymes from raw foods, will eventually run out causing disease and pre-mature aging.[8] Enzymes in food are denatured at a degree ranging from 110-115, so cooked foods offer none to aid in their digestion. The body must use its own enzymes to process cooked food.[9]

Heating food also alters nutritional content. All food starts out living and the further it gets from this state, the less it nourishes the body. For example, vitamins, carbohydrates, proteins, and fats are all organic molecules and break down when exposed to heat, light, and air. This break down causes a drastic loss in nutritional value and the longer the exposure, the greater the loss.[10]

Why do these different types of vegans subscribe to the lifestyle?

*"If we are to nurture our culture, let's begin with the animals who have been nothing but our beasts of burden for so long."*
*-Rikki Rocket, drummer for Poison[11]*

Several reasons:

## PERSONAL HEALTH

Choosing a plant-based diet has incredible health benefits including less incidence of disease, lower blood pressure and cholesterol, lower BMI (Body Mass Index) and improved overall health.[12] There are several major reasons why a vegan diet improves health.

> *"Thou should eat to live; not live to eat."*
> *-Socrates, Greek Philosopher*[13]

First, consuming animal products is one of the most damaging choices that you can make for your health. Meat and dairy contain dietary cholesterol, considerable saturated fat, no fiber, and compared to plants, very little vitamins and minerals. The saving grace of meat is that it contains a "complete" protein, but read ahead... studies show that plant proteins are actually easier for the body to use.[14]

There is also the issue of the disease, parasites, pesticides, antibiotics, and other toxicities found in animal flesh.[15] Consumers tend to forget that when eating an animal, they are exposing themselves to all to which that animal was exposed. Living conditions of all farmed animals, including those raised "organically" or "humanely" are atrocious.[16] Most are diseased, pumped full of antibiotics and hormones, and fed cheap grains covered in pesticides. These chemicals are stored in the animal's tissues and passed on to the consumer.[17] These dangers are present in fish, poultry, pork, and red meat but appear in greater concentrations in larger animals who have lived longer and have stored more in their tissues.

There are also post-slaughter additives that pose a great threat to the consumer. Chemicals like Nitrates, Hydrocarbons, and Malonaldehyde, are used in cured meats, charcoal broiling, and rancidity testing, respectively, and are directly ingested with the meat product.[18]

What does all of this mean for the meat eater? Cancer, liver and kidney disease, heart disease, stroke, and obesity to name a few.[19] Not to mention lower quality of life and damaged body aesthetics. Please remember that no animal flesh, even chicken or fish, is free from chemical exposure. And all are more difficult for the body to digest.

> *"Everybody is a genius. But if you judge a fish by its ability to climb a tree, it will live its whole life believing that it is stupid."*
> *-Albert Einstein*[20]

Dairy products are equally, if not more, damaging to health than meat. Humans are the only animal species that continue to drink milk after weaning; and the only one that will consume another animal's milk. Milk is only meant as a first food with fat and calorie proportions meant for rapid growth and development.

Cow's milk is the most commonly consumed, most likely because of the size of the animal and the quantity of milk that they produce. But that's a disturbing conundrum: their milk is meant to nourish a calf to an eventual weight in the thousands of pounds in a matter of months. What does this mean for humans, meant to be 200 pounds at the most, who consume cow's milk?

Damaged body aesthetics, for starters. Milk is loaded with fat and calories that will absolutely contribute to weight gain. It also causes inflammation in the body, which can lead to countless issues, including acne and other skin disorders. Dairy products are a disaster for your physical appearance.

And the consequences of consuming dairy are beyond skin deep. A significant percentage of the population suffers from Lactose Intolerance, the inability to digest lactose, a sugar in cow's milk. Newborn babies are born with lactase, an enzyme produced in the small intestine needed to digest milk. Because we are only meant to drink our mother's milk during the early years of our lives, it makes sense that we would stop producing this enzyme as we mature.[22] Symptoms of lactose intolerance include gas, diarrhea, and bloating. Pretty gross.

There are also components of cow's milk that the immune system recognizes as dangerous, which leads to the release of body chemicals that fight allergens. This defensive immune reaction is what leads to inflammation, which causes, among other things, the over production of mucous, joint pain, and skin conditions like psoriasis.[23]

> *"A man can live and be healthy without killing animals for food; therefor, if he eats meat, he participates in taking animal life merely for the sake of his appetite. And to act so is immoral."*
> *-Leo Tolstoy, Russian Novelist*[25]

Vegans only eat plant-based foods, including vegetables, fruits, beans, grains, legumes, and nuts, all of which are high in vitamins, minerals, fiber, and antioxidants. They contain protein, very little saturated fat, and very little cholesterol. Plants are the source of energy for all animals on Earth.

Look at it this way: all of the energy that life on the planet needs comes from the sun. Plants absorb this energy and through photosynthesis feed themselves. Then animals, including humans, eat the plants to receive the harvested energy. When animals eat other animals they are receiving that energy secondhand. By directly eating the plants and their fruits, vegans receive the sun's energy from a more direct source.[26]

And because vegans eat lower on the food chain, they are exposed to significantly less chemical pesticides and fertilizers. Vegetables, fruits, and grains contain only 11% of the chemical residues found in the American diet; the rest are found in meat and dairy.[27] Not only are vegans ingesting considerably less toxic chemicals, they are consuming more antioxidants, which fight the diseases caused by free radicals, most notably cancer.

Free radicals also lead to premature aging, so consuming antioxidant-rich plants helps preserve youth. And because plant foods are high in fiber and low in calories and fat, they help keep you thin.

Despite these benefits, the vegan diet is often criticized for being deficient and unhealthy. While it is absolutely possible to eat an unbalanced plant-based diet, one that is well-managed is beyond healthful.[28]

Vegans are most often questioned about their protein intake because of the common misconception that animal protein is the best source. Proteins are made up of 20 amino acids, 11 of which the human body produces. That means we must ingest the remaining 9, the essential amino acids, from our food.[29] Animal products contain protein strands similar to ours, so are considered "complete;" but these proteins must first be broken down into the component amino acids and then re-synthesized into proteins that we can use. This uses a lot of energy.[30]

Plants contain all 20 amino acids and are only considered incomplete because they are low in one or two of the essential amino acids.[31] Think of it like a coin counter: when various plant foods are metabolized the amino acids are distributed into each "slot," and when each is full, a protein is synthesized. Eating a variety of plant foods provides more than enough of each amino acid to produce all of the protein that we need, even those who lead active lives.

## ANIMAL RIGHTS

*"The time will come when men will look upon the murder of animals as they look upon the murder of men"*
*-Leonardo Da Vinci, Italian Renaissance Artist* [32]

Animal rights is likely the first thing that comes to mind when the word "vegan" is mentioned. The belief in compassion for all living things is the basic premise of veganism and is probably the most common reason people consider this lifestyle. To understand the vegan passion for protecting all life by not only removing animal products from their diets, but also from their lifestyles, one must face some uncomfortable realities. The pork on your plate was once a pig and the leather on your shoes once covered a cow's flesh. It's important to realize what those animals experienced to get on your plate and around your feet.

*"SPECIEISM: a prejudice or attitude of bias in favor of the interests of one's own species and against those of another species."*
*-from Earthlings, 2005 animal rights documentary* [33]

Because humans have deemed themselves superior to all other species on the planet, we exploit other animals for our appetites, conveniences, and amusement at the expense of their freedom and wellness.[34] And we do so in such a way that the majority of us don't have to consider the implications of our consumption. Lifestyle Vegans do not participate in any form of animal exploitation, including zoos, circuses, or animal races, and avoid all products, including drugs, cosmetics, and household cleaners that have been tested on animals.

*"You have just dined and however scrupulously the slaughterhouse is concealed in the graceful distance of miles, there is complicity"*
*-Ralph Waldo Emerson, American Transcendentalist writer* [35]

Most animals consumed in America were raised and slaughtered on factory farms. It is no coincidence that slaughterhouses have no windows and are located in the middle of nowhere.

Animals are crammed into small spaces, disallowed to participate in instinctual acts, and injected with chemicals to expedite their growth.[36] They are then transported to assembly-lined slaughterhouses where they are mechanically killed and processed. There are no animal cruelty laws to protect animals produced for food so there is no limit to the inhumanities that they experience.[37] Dairy cows and hens endure as much or more cruelty as animals killed for their flesh. They are bled dry of their milk and eggs and cruelly discarded when they have been used to their capacity.[38]

> *"The Gods created certain kinds of beings to replenish our bodies: they are the trees and the plants and the seeds"*
> *-Plato, Greek Philosopher*[39]

Leather, fur, wool, and silk are all produced at the expense of an animal's comfort and life. Animals raised and slaughtered for their fur, skin, and products are treated as inhumanly as those killed for their flesh. Lifestyle Vegans feel it is just as significant and unsavory to wear or use an animal product as it is to consume one as food.

Understanding the implications of wearing leather and fur are easy; but the abuse behind the consumption of silk and wool products are equally disturbing and often ignored.

Wool is made from the fleece of sheep, who if left in their natural states produce just enough wool to insulate their bodies. But humans who stand to make money off of these animals have used genetic engineering and selective breeding to create sheep that produce way more than needed.[40] Sheep are abused, mutilated, and most often end up slaughtered for their meat. Wearing wool leaves the same residue of blood on the consumer's hands as wearing leather and fur.

The standards for animal products labeled "organic" and "humanely raised" are only slightly different than conventional products and should not be considered compassionate consumption.[41] There is, after all, nothing humane about slaughter or exploitation.

> *"Those who, by their purchases, require animals to be killed have no right to be shielded from the slaughterhouses or any other aspect of the production of the meat they buy. If it is distasteful for humans to think about, what can it be like for the animals who experience it?"*
> *-Peter Singer, Australian Philosopher*[42]

Silk is also produced at the expense of another species' comfort and life. Silk worms produce a protein substance that hardens into silk fibers. The silk is harvested from the worm's cocoon, killing the worm in the process. The extraction processes can be very cruel, including boiling, baking, and steaming live cocoons. Moths are genetically modified to prohibit flight and females are killed after laying their eggs; and males after mating.[43]

> " Life is God's or Nature's greatest gift. All life should be treated with respect and dignity."
> - Geezer Butler, bass player for Black Sabbath[44]

# ENVIRONMENTAL

This may come as a surprise, but meat consumption, especially in the United States, is significantly disastrous to the environment. Meat production causes a domino effect that affects global warming, rainforest deforestation, and animal extinction.[45]

To understand the correlation you must first consider the amount of U.S. farmland that is currently devoted to animals raised as food. In the United States, over half of the land devoted to agriculture is already used for their grazing and food. Overproducing mineral-leaching crops like corn, soy, and oats for their food is causing massive topsoil erosion and mineral depletion. And to make up for the resulting poor soil quality, harmful chemical fertilizers are used. Forests are also being destroyed for fresh farmland. This contributes further to topsoil erosion and removes trees, which are valuable to the removal of atmospheric Carbon Dioxide, one of the most significant greenhouse gases.[46]

Just as fast as Americans are destroying their forests, Central and South America are clearing more land to raise livestock to sell to the United States. Unfortunately for all of us, that land is mostly rainforest.[47] Thirty percent of the world's forests, rainforests account for 80% of the world's land vegetation. They are also home to unique animal and plant species, which are in danger of extinction. The South American cattle producers also burn the rainforests to clear the land, releasing more greenhouse gases and further contributing to global warming.[48]

> "Earth provides enough to satisfy every man's need, but not every man's greed."
> - Mohandas Gandhi, Indian Political Leaders[49]

Then there's the water. It takes 25 gallons of water to produce one pound of wheat and 2500 gallons to produce one pound of meat. More than half of the water currently used in the United States is devoted to livestock.[50] And that's not even the worst part. Producing livestock requires enormous amounts of chemical pesticides and fertilizers, which end up polluting our water. And because animals are raised in such large numbers, the waste they produce is far too much to be recycled. It either poisons the land or runs off into our water.[51] Feedlots are a more significant source of river pollution than the byproducts of industry.[52]

The process of converting the proteins in plants to animal protein is very inefficient and taxing on the planet. The same acre used to produce one pound of meat, if planted with protein-rich plant foods, could sustain 15 people.[53] Vegetarian foods create less than 5% of the strain on the planet than meat and dairy products.[54] There is more than enough land to feed the world but the disproportionate demand for animal products is straining the Earth beyond its capacity.

*"For as long as men massacre animals, they will kill each other. Indeed, he who sows the seed of murder and pain cannot reap joy and love."*
*- Pythagoras, Greek Philosopher[55]*

Becoming a vegan is a journey. Any change in consciousness regarding your personal health, the health of the environment, and/or the rights of animals should be applauded. The above information is only meant to inform you about the different perceptions of what it means to be a vegan and the different reasons people choose the vegan lifestyle so that you can participate in whichever way you feel comfortable.

Now that you know why people choose a vegan diet, it's time to learn how to participate. Preparing vegan food can be just as easy as preparing conventional food; it just takes a different understanding. And some different kitchen staples.

You'll be surprised at how easy it is to create the same foods that you're used to without using animal products. With a better understanding of the functions of eggs, milk, and butter in cooking and baking, you'll see that they are easily and effectively replaced with plant foods, creating a much healthier and equally appealing product.

Eggs provide several functions in prepared foods (especially baked goods), so there are several substitutes to accommodate each role that they play. The coagulated proteins in eggs, both the yolks and whites, provide structure in cake-like baked goods. Eggs also thicken custards and creams, assist in the leavening process, emulsify by binding oil and water, and add moisture.[56]

The chart below illustrates general vegan substitutions for each of these roles.

| FUNCTION | VEGAN SUBSTITUTION (PER EGG) |
|----------|------------------------------|
| Custard/Creams | 1 tablespoon arrowroot powder |
| Leavening | 1 tsp baking powder + 1 tsp vinegar |
| Emulsifier | 1 tablespoon arrowroot powder |
| Moisture | 2 ounces almond or rice milk |

The main function of milk is to add moisture. Using nut or rice milk almost always provides the same result. The only exception is whipped cream. Plant-based milks will not thicken when whipped. There are, however, other methods to create cream-like products.

Butter just serves as a fat when cooking. Believe it or not, this is the easiest animal product to replace. The mostly unsaturated fats from plant oils provide the same function in baking and cooking. And there are many plant-based flavorings that simulate the taste of butter.

## ALWAYS ORGANIC

It goes without saying that every ingredient called for in our recipes should be organic. To save ink and paper, we aren't going to print the word, "organic," before each. We are instead going to explain now just how important purchasing organic goods is for your health and the health of the planet.

Fruits and vegetables raised conventionally contain residues of up to 67 different chemical pesticides and fertilizers.[57] Studies show that these chemicals can have severe effects on neurological and endocrine function and development, especially in children.[58] Common sense tells us that any chemical meant to kill any living thing will likely have negative effects on our own living bodies. And pesticide residues are thought to contribute to Attention Deficit Disorder, cancer, immune system deficiency, and nervous system disorders.[59]

USDA organic standards prohibit certain farming techniques that leach the soil of valuable minerals. Organic crops must be rotated and green manures used to replenish the land. Our crops are only as nutritious as the soil they are grown in, and organic produce is higher in vitamins and minerals.[60]

These organic methods, along with the use of eco-friendly fertilizers and insect control contribute to environmental sustainment. The dangerous and abrasive chemicals used in conventional farming are detrimental to the planet. They pollute the water, create negative chain reactions in the eco-system, and leave unhealthy residues in the soil.[61] Consuming food grown under USDA organic standards drastically reduces harmful chemical contamination.

The Environmental Protection Agency (EPA) regulates the kinds and amounts of pesticides used on food crops through required laboratory tests, which determine how these chemicals will affect humans. While the EPA has made efforts to reduce animal testing, there are still required tests conducted on animals that expose them to deadly and abrasive chemicals to record their consumption capacity.[62] Consuming conventional produce and products contributes to the torture and untimely death of animals.

*"The love for all living creatures is the most notable attribute of man."*
*- Charles Darwin, English Naturalist*[63]

We know that the "organic" label has been abused. But regardless of how flawed the system governing organic standards is, please remember that consuming any conventional product is participating in the destruction of the environment and your personal health. Attempting to outsmart nature has only led to irreparable damage to the world around us. The only way to mitigate this damage is by adopting methods that attempt to work with the environment instead of against. Organic food growth and production is less demanding on our world and reduces damage to air quality, our water supply, the land, and our own bodies.

## NO SOY

As you browse our recipes, you're going to notice that none call for soy products. For starters, foods like tofu and tempeh are what have given the vegan diet a bad name. Soy "meats" and "cheeses" are terrible. And are also not good for you. These products are very processed. Look at a soybean: it's green. How does that bean turn into a white block?

It is because of soy's protein content that vegans have historically relied on it to produce substitutes; this has been a mistake. Soy contains potent anti-nutrients that prohibit nutrient absorption and can lead to a host of diseases. Countless studies have linked soy to endocrine dysfunction, heart disease, cancer, and decreased immune function.[65] Considering soy a health food is a mistake that can result in disaster for your body.

Soy-based vegan meat and dairy substitutes have never made sense to us, so we came up with our own fresh and organic recipes that give the same sensation of meat and dairy products. We spent great time developing recipes that are not only healthful, but will satisfy the cravings of even non-vegans. All of our recipes call for organic vegetables and grains and can be made in bulk and refrigerated or frozen for later use.

# VEGAN PANTRY

Vegan pantry items will probably, at first, seem unfamiliar. It will take getting used to, but once you are familiarized with plant-based products, it will become second nature to include them on your shopping list. Below, we have outlined the staples of the vegan pantry, briefing their role in the process, and exposing where they can be purchased.

### ALMOND MILK

Almond milk is made from grinding soaked almonds with water and then straining and removing the fiber. It is an ideal milk substitute and can be found in health food stores and most grocery outlets. Make sure to read the ingredients: almond milk is often sweetened and flavored with vanilla. If using in a recipe, purchase unsweetened almond milk with no vanilla.

### APPLE CIDER VINEGAR

Apple cider vinegar is made from the fermentation of apples and is thought to contribute to weight loss and aid in the treatment of a slew of common ailments. Although white vinegar can be used with the same result, we recommend using apple cider vinegar. It can be found at almost any market.

### ARROWROOT POWDER

Extracted from the roots of tropical plants, arrowroot is used as a thickener or binder in vegan food. Arrowroot contains trace amounts of vitamins and minerals and is low in calories. It can be found at health food stores and some specialty markets.

### BAKING POWDER

Baking powder is a leavening agent made from baking soda, acid salt, and a filler, such as, cornstarch. When dissolved in water, the baking soda and acids combine to form carbon dioxide gas, which leavens.[67] Make sure to purchase non-aluminum baking powder: aluminum is toxic when ingested. Non-aluminum baking powder can be found at almost any market.

### BAKING SODA

Baking Soda, or sodium bicarbonate, releases carbon dioxide gas when exposed to moisture and heat. It is most often used as an accompaniment to baking powder.[68] Baking soda can be found at any market.

### BROWN RICE

Brown Rice is rice with only the outer "husk" removed, preserving the grain's significant nutritional value. There are many varieties of brown rice but those most commonly found at health food stores and markets are small, medium, and long grain. Long grain rice is the least mushy when cooked and is the best option when using as a base for stir-fries or rice sides.[69] Medium and short-grain brown rice are gummy and are ideal for blended recipes. Brown rice can be found at almost every grocery store or market.

## CHICKPEA (GARBANZO BEAN) FLOUR
Made from ground chickpeas, this is a staple gluten-free flour. High in protein and strong in flavor, it is included in most gluten-free mixes. Chickpea flour can be found at health food stores.

## EVAPORATED CANE JUICE (OR ORGANIC SUGAR)
It is very important to always use organic, unbleached granulated sugar. Evaporated cane juice uses less energy to produce, so it's our first recommendation. Organic sugar and evaporated cane juice can be found at health food stores and most supermarkets.

## GRAPE SEED OIL
Not only is grape seed oil high in antioxidants, its high smoking point makes it ideal for sautéing. It's also great in baked goods. Grape seed oil can be found at health food stores and most markets.

## HIMALAYAN PINK SALT
All of our recipes call for Himalayan pink salt. It is pure, full of minerals, and contains great nutritional value. It can be found at health food stores and some markets.

## NUTRITIONAL YEAST
Nutritional yeast is made by culturing yeast on sugar cane or beet molasses. It is killed with heat (deactivated), and typically fortified with B12. It has a cheese-like flavor and is used to make vegan cheese substitutes. It is also high in vitamins, minerals, and protein. Nutritional yeast can be found in health food stores.

## ORGANIC VEGETABLE SHORTENING
Organic shortening is made from plant oils. It has the texture of conventional shortening but has not been hydrogenated. This is an excellent butter substitute. Organic shortening can be found at health food stores and some conventional markets.

## RICE MILK
Rice Milk is made by blending soaked rice with water and then straining and removing the fiber. It is a good vegan milk for those with nut allergies. Rice milk can be found in almost any grocery store or market.

## SORGHUM FLOUR
Sorghum is a cereal grain often used in gluten-free flour mixes. It offers nutritional benefits but must be mixed with other flours, as is doesn't embody all that is needed for a baking flour. Sorghum flour can be found in health food stores.

## UNBLEACHED WHITE FLOUR
Unbleached white flour is made from the ground endosperm portion of the wheat berry. Conventional white flours are bleached with chemicals and often enriched. White wheat flour is much more tender and produces softer baked goods. It is less nutritious and if you choose this flour, make sure it is unbleached, unbromated, and organic. Unbleached white flour can be found at any market.

## WHOLE WHEAT FLOUR
Whole wheat flour contains the fiber and nutrients of the entire wheat berry and is the more nutritious wheat flour choice. It is more course and will produce a more dense baked good. We recommend reducing flour volume when using whole wheat (adjustments included in each recipe). Whole wheat flour can be found at any market.

## VEGAN CHOCOLATE CHIPS
Vegan chocolate chips are made without milk or other animal additives. It is very important to purchase those marked "vegan," as animal products are sometimes used as emulsifiers. Vegan chocolate chips can be found in health food stores and some specialty markets.

## YEAST
Yeast is a microbial fungus that converts sugars in dough to carbon dioxide through fermentation. The gas causes the dough to expand and rise. Yeast can be found at any grocery store or market.

## XANTHAN GUM
Xanthan gum is made from the fermentation of the microorganism, xanthomonas campestris. It is a thickener often used in salad dressings and baked goods.[70] It is a necessary component in gluten-free baking.

"Meatballs" (page 40)

# SYMBOL SYSTEM

You'll notice that we've assigned each frequently used recipe a symbol. This is the basis of our program. Making fresh, organic, and nutritious food requires some extra work. But our symbol system will allow you to make the most of your efforts.

We are asking you to prepare items that you are probably used to buying already made. We get it. But making your own food is the only way to ensure that you are eating the right things. And once you get the hang of it, it will be second nature to produce these recipes in bulk to use throughout the week.

Using the symbols is easy: Just look at the bottom of the recipe to see the symbols of the included basic recipes. Then search other recipes to find another that uses the basic ingredient that you have already prepared.

We recommend making these frequently used recipes in bulk and freezing.

 PUREED EGGPLANT

 WHITE BEANS

 FIRM "CHEESE"

 HAMBURGER BUNS

 SOFT "CHEESE"

 TORTILLAS

 EGGPLANT BURGERS

 PIZZA DOUGH

 "SAUSAGE"

 PIE CRUST

 "MEATBALLS"

 FRESH HERB MARINARA

 VEGETABLE STOCK

 CASHEW "CREAM"

 BROWN RICE

 TAHINI

 BLACK BEANS

 "CUSTARD"

There has been a nationwide nutritional witch-hunt over the last several years creating a marketing frenzy for gluten-free products. But what exactly is the target?

Gluten is a protein found in wheat, rye, and barley that is responsible for the elastic-like quality of bread dough and baking batters. It is the reason why wheat has been used as flour for centuries. Gluten itself isn't present in the wheat flour: the protein substances glutenin and gliadin form gluten when water is added. The gluten continually changes as it is handled, becoming stronger and more stretchy. This is why we knead bread dough; it brings out the gluten, binding the dough.[71]

So what's the harm in this age-old foodstuff? Not much unless you are one out of every 133 Americans who has been diagnosed with Celiac Disease or gluten intolerance. Those affected have a reaction to gluten that causes the intestinal villa to flatten, which prevents the absorption of nutrients from food. Symptoms include weight loss, diarrhea, and potential malnutrition.[72]

The only treatment for Celiac is total avoidance of wheat, rye, barley, and their byproducts. This can be extremely expensive. Gluten-free flours and the additives that make them suitable for baking are costly. To make a grain-flour that doesn't contain gluten ready to use for baking, a starch and a binder must be added. These are expensive.

There are several options for gluten-free flours including rice, amaranth, sorghum, and garbanzo bean. And there are many gluten-free baking mixes available at health food stores. These contain thoughtful blends of gluten-free flours, which contain appropriate proteins for baking quality while considering flavors.

To be fair we must mention that there is an opposing view. As we mentioned, only one in every 133 Americans has been diagnosed with Celiac, but it has become a marketing frenzy. The label "gluten-free" has been plastered on everything, including foods that have never historically contained wheat, rye, or barley.[73]

Gluten-free does not necessarily mean "healthy;" and there are health benefits to all whole grains. With that being said, we provide gluten-free substitutions and explanations for all recipes, so if you are seeking this lifestyle, you will be able to do so without the use of animal products.

# GLUTEN-FREE BASICS

## NO NEED TO KNEAD

Kneading is the process of working doughs made from wheat flour to release the gluten. This step should obviously be skipped when making gluten-free breads. Instead, doughs should be beaten, or vigorously stirred, to fully incorporate the binders. Two minutes is the recommended beating time

## ADJUST YOUR EXPECTATIONS

Adjust your expectations of what doughs and batters should look like. Gluten is what gives conventional dough its smooth and elastic consistency; bread doughs made with gluten-free flours are much softer, closer to the texture of cookie dough. Batters and doughs are also more grainy.

Please also keep in mind, gluten-free flours rise and expand differently. Expect a smaller and more dense finished product.

## CAREFULLY MEASURE

The use of of a binder in gluten-free baking is imperative, but mis measuring can lead to disaster. Too much will create a dense and gummy end-product and too little, one that won't hold together. Make sure to measure correctly.

Here is our recipe for an all purpose gluten-free flour.

We chose nutrient-rich flours with mild flavors so that the taste of your baked goods will not be sacrificed. This flour alone will not hold up in recipes; the appropriate amount of binder must be added depending on the desired texture. We recommend xanthan gum.

The chart below will give you an idea of how much to use for each type of baked good using our gluten-free flour blend. These suggested quantities are ONLY recommended for use with our gluten-free flour mix. If using a packaged mix, please use the manufacturer's binder recommendations.

You can find gluten-free substitutions at the bottom of each recipe containing gluten in this format:

GLUTEN-FREE | xx GLUTEN-FREE FLOUR MIX | xx XANTHUM GUM

# GLUTEN-FREE ALL PURPOSE FLOUR

### YIELD: 1 CUP

**3 tablespoons sorghum flour**
**3 tablespoons chickpea flour**
**3 tablespoons brown rice flour**
**⅓ cup arrowroot powder**
**¼ teaspoon sugar**

Combine ingredients and store in an airtight container.

| FOOD | XANTHAN GUM PER CUP FLOUR |
|:---:|:---:|
| Muffins | ¼ teaspoon |
| Breads | ¼ teaspoon |
| Pizza Crust | 1 teaspoon |
| Cookies | ⅛ teaspoon |
| Cakes | ¼ -½ teaspoon |

# BASICS

# FIRM CHEESE
YIELD: 16 OUNCE BLOCK

¼ cup shortening
¼ cup arrowroot powder
1 cup almond or rice milk
4 cups nutritional yeast

Melt shortening in a medium saucepan over medium heat. Mix in arrowroot with a spatula until incorporated. Whisk in almond milk until smooth. Continue to stir until thick (should be the consistency of paste).

Add nutritional yeast one cup at a time. When the mixture becomes too thick to stir, knead remaining nutritional yeast into "cheese" until all is incorporated.

Press into a glass container or bowl. Cover and refrigerate for at least one hour. "Cheese" will be fully hardened and ready to shave, grate, or cut after 12 hours.

Refrigerate in an airtight container for up to one week. Can be frozen for up to three months

# SOFT CHEESE
YIELD: 2 CUPS

3 tablespoons grape seed oil
¼ cup flour (¼ cup whole wheat)
1 cup almond or rice milk
2 cups nutritional yeast

Combine grape seed oil and flour in a medium saucepan over medium-high heat.

Whisk in almond milk until smooth.

Stir in nutritional yeast.

Refrigerate in an airtight container for up to one week. Can be frozen for up to three months.

GLUTEN-FREE | 5 tbsp GLUTEN-FREE FLOUR MIX

# PUREED EGGPLANT

YIELD: 2-3 CUPS

**1 medium eggplant**
**¼ cup grape seed oil**

Preheat oven to 425 degrees.

Remove the top of the eggplant and cut lengthways into ¼-inch slices.

Cover a 9x13-inch baking dish with foil and grease with 2 tablespoons of grape seed oil.

Toss eggplant slices in the remaining grape seed oil making sure all areas are covered.

Place in preheated oven and roast until tender, about 30-45 minutes.

In food processor (with S blade) or blender, puree roasted eggplant until smooth.

Refrigerate in an airtight container for up to one week. Can be frozen for up to three months.

EGGPLANT is the base for several of our "meat" substitutes, not only because of its rich flavors, but also its rich nutritional content. Eggplant is high in antioxidants, potassium, and vitamins B1 and B6. It contains significant amounts of copper, magnesium, folic acid, and niacin.[74]

# EGGPLANT BURGER

YIELD: 6 PATTIES

1 tablespoon grape seed oil
1 cup mushrooms, sliced
2 cloves garlic, chopped
1 cup Pureed Eggplant
1 tablespoon apple cider vinegar
1 teaspoon pink salt
1 teaspoon dried fennel
1 tablespoon dried marjoram
1 tablespoon fresh thyme (1 tsp dried thyme)
¼ cup arrowroot powder
2 tablespoons flour (2 tbsp whole wheat)
1½ cups cooked brown rice

Preheat oven to 400 degrees.

In a small skillet over medium-high heat, saute mushrooms and 1 clove garlic in grape seed oil until tender (about 5 minutes).

In a food processor (with S blade) or blender, blend Pureed Eggplant, mushroom mixture, remaining garlic, vinegar, salt, fennel, marjoram, and thyme.

Add arrowroot and flour and blend until incorporated.

Add brown rice and blend until smooth.

Form into 6 patties on parchment-lined baking sheet.

Bake in preheated oven for 40-45 minutes.

Refrigerate in an airtight container for up to one week. Can be frozen for up to three months.

GLUTEN-FREE | 3 tbsp GLUTEN-FREE FLOUR MIX

# EGGPLANT "SAUSAGE"
YIELD: 12 PATTIES

1½ cups Pureed Eggplant
1 clove garlic
1 teaspoon apple cider vinegar
1 teaspoon pink salt
1 tablespoon dried fennel
1 teaspoon dried marjoram
1 tablespoon fresh thyme (1 tsp dried thyme)
½ teaspoon sage
¼ cup arrowroot powder
2 tablespoons flour (2 tbsp whole wheat)
2 cups cooked brown rice
1½ teaspoons crushed red pepper

Preheat oven to 400 degrees.

In a food processor (with S blade) or blender, blend Pureed Eggplant, garlic, vinegar, pink salt, fennel, marjoram, thyme, and sage.

Add arrowroot and flour and blend until incorporated.

Add brown rice and blend until smooth. Fold in red pepper flakes.

Form into 12 patties on parchment-lined baking sheet.

Bake in preheated oven for 40-45 minutes.

Refrigerate in an airtight container for up to one week. Can be frozen for up to three months.

GLUTEN-FREE | 3 tbsp GLUTEN-FREE FLOUR MIX

# "MEATBALLS"
YIELD: ABOUT 30 BALLS

1 cup Pureed Eggplant
1 clove garlic, minced
2 tablespoons nutritional yeast
¼ cup arrowroot powder
2 tablespoons flour (2 tbsp whole wheat)
1 tablespoon chopped fresh oregano (1 tsp dried oregano)
1 tablespoon chopped fresh thyme (½ tsp dried thyme)
1 teaspoon marjoram
½ teaspoon pink salt
1 cup cooked brown rice
¼ cup minced red onion
1 tablespoon chopped fresh parsley

Preheat oven to 375 degrees.

In a food processor (with S blade) or blender, blend Pureed Eggplant, garlic, nutritional yeast, arrowroot, oregano, thyme, marjoram, and pink salt.

Blend in brown rice until smooth. Fold in red onion and parsley.

Spoon tablespoon-sized balls onto a parchment-lined baking sheet.

Bake in preheated oven for 25-30 minutes.

Refrigerate in an airtight container for up to one week. Can be frozen for up to three months.

GLUTEN-FREE | 3 tbsp GLUTEN-FREE FLOUR MIX

# VEGETABLE STOCK 🍲

YIELD: ABOUT 10 CUPS

I medium red onion, chopped
3 cloves garlic, crushed
1 medium carrot, chopped
2 ribs celery, chopped
½ cup chopped mushrooms
2 bay leaves
4 sprigs fresh thyme
½ cup chopped parsley
1 teaspoon pink salt
1 teaspoon black pepper
10 cups water

Place all ingredients into a large stock pot and bring to a boil.

Reduce heat to low, cover, and simmer for one hour.

Turn off the heat and let sit for an additional hour.

Refrigerate with solids for up to two weeks.

## BOUILLON PASTE

In a food processor (with S blade) or blender, blend all solids until smooth.

Refrigerate in an airtight container for up to two weeks. Can be frozen for up to three months.

1 tbsp BOUILLON PASTE + 1 CUP WATER = 1 CUP STOCK

# CASHEW CREAM
YIELD: 1 CUP

**1 cup whole raw cashews**
**¾ cup water**
**¼ teaspoon pink salt**

Place cashews, water, and pink salt in the container of a high-powered blender.

Blend until smooth.

Refrigerate in an airtight container for up to one week. Can be frozen for up to three months.

If using cashew pieces, use 1 cup of water.

# RAW TAHINI
YIELD: 4 CUPS

**5 cups sesame seeds**
**3½ cups water**

Place sesame seeds and water in the container of a high-powered blender.

Blend until smooth.

Refrigerate in an airtight container for up to one week. Can be frozen for up to three months.

# BROWN RICE
YIELD: 4 CUPS

I cup brown rice
2½ cups water
½ teaspoon pink salt

Place rice, water, and pink salt into a medium saucepan.

Bring to a boil.

Reduce heat to low, cover, and simmer for 30-35 minutes.


# QUINOA
YIELD: 4 CUPS

1 cup quinoa
2 cups water
¼ teaspoon pink salt

Place quinoa, water, and pink salt into a medium saucepan.

Bring to a boil.

Reduce heat to low, cover, and simmer for 15 minutes.


# LENTILS
YIELD: ABOUT 2 CUPS

1 cup lentils
2 cups water
¼ teaspoon pink salt

Place lentils and water into a medium saucepan.

Bring to a light simmer.

Reduce heat to low and simmer uncovered until tender (about 15-20 minutes).

Add pink salt.

# BEANS
YIELD: 4 CUPS

**1 cup dried beans, rinsed and soaked**
**3 cups water**

Place soaked beans and water into a large saucepan.

Bring to a boil.

Reduce heat, cover, and simmer until tender (1-1½ hours).

---

SOAK BEANS
Carefully rinse 1 cup of dried beans. Place into a bowl and cover with 3 cups of fresh water.

Soak for at least six hours.

Drain and rinse.

---

It is always best to use fresh beans. Of course, canned beans may be substituted in our recipes, but nothing compares to fresh ingredients. All of the beans in our recipes are cooked in the same way.
Beans can be cooked in bulk and frozen for later use.

We have assigned symbols for the most commonly used beans in our recipes.

 BLACK BEANS        WHITE BEANS

# BREADS and CRACKERS

# BREAD MAKING BASICS

## KNEADING

Kneading is the process of working dough made with wheat flour in order to release the gluten. This creates smooth and elastic dough and a soft bread. Dough is typically flipped onto a floured board and continuously folded and worked back into itself with the palms of the hands for 5-10 minutes.

We aren't going to lie to you. A standing mixer makes the process of making bread a lot easier. There is an attachment called a "dough hook" that actually kneads the bread for you. But if you don't have one, don't worry. You can make it just as well by hand. Just make sure to reduce flour by ¼ cup when mixing dough and add (as needed) while kneading.

## CUTTING

Cutting is the gentle incorporation of shortening into the dry ingredients of certain doughs, mainly biscuits and flaky pastries. This is typically done with a pastry blender, a horseshoe-shaped kitchen utensil that shaves the shortening into the flour. You may also "cut" shortening into the flour mixture using your fingers. The key to cutting shortening, though, is to not over do it. The shortening should be JUST incorporated and the mixture should appear crumbly. Overworking biscuit and pastry dough will produce a tough baked good. And that's bad.

## RISING

All dough made with yeast requires time to rise, usually 1½- 2½ hours. This allows the yeast to ferment and create $CO_2$ gas, which causes the dough to expand. Breads and rolls typically rise twice. After the first rise, you "punch" the dough to release some of the gas so that it can be shaped. Then the prepared dough is left to rise again creating a light finished product.

# BURGER BUNS

YIELD: 12 LARGE OR 24 MINI BUNS

**1 cup almond milk**
**1 cup water**
**2 tablespoons shortening**
**1 tablespoon sugar**
**5 cups flour** (4½ cups wheat flour)
**1 package yeast**
**1 teaspoon baking powder**
**1½ teaspoons pink salt**
**1 teaspoon vinegar**

In a medium saucepan over medium-high heat, combine almond milk, water, sugar, and shortening and bring to a boil.

Remove from heat and allow to cool to room temperature.

Mix flour, yeast, baking powder, and pink salt in a large mixing bowl. Add lukewarm almond mixture and vinegar and mix until incorporated. Using the dough hook on a standing mixer, or your hands on a floured board, knead the dough for 8 minutes. Dough should be smooth and elastic.

Place into a greased bowl and flip to cover all sides. Cover and allow to rise in a warm, dark place until doubled in size (about one hour).

Punch dough and divide into 12 equal pieces (24 if making mini buns).

Make an OK sign with your thumb and forefinger and press dough pieces through to create smooth balls, pinching and twisting the excess on the bottom to keep the dough taut. Place on a parchment-lined baking sheet and flatten with the palm of your hand into 4-inch circles (2-inch for mini buns)•. Repeat until all buns are made.

Preheat oven to 400 degrees.

Cover and allow to rise for an additional 30 minutes.

Bake for 10 minutes in preheated oven.

---

GLUTEN-FREE | 5¼ CUPS GLUTEN-FREE FLOUR MIX | ¾ tsp XANTHAN GUM

---

•SUB ROLLS | GENTLY ROLL DOUGH BALLS BETWEEN YOUR PALMS UNTIL ABOUT 6 INCHES LONG

# PIZZA DOUGH
YIELD: 2 12-INCH OR 4 6-INCH CRUSTS

¼ cup warm water
1 package yeast
2 cups flour (1¾ cups whole wheat)
1 teaspoon pink salt
½ cup cool water
2 tablespoons chopped fresh basil (1 tbsp dried basil)
1 tablespoon chopped fresh oregano (1 tsp dried oregano)
2 tablespoons grape seed oil

In a large mixing bowl, combine ¼ cup warm water, yeast, and ¼ cup flour, until smooth.

Cover and allow to rise for 15 minutes.

Add remaining flour, pink salt, cool water, basil, and oregano and mix until incorporated. Using the dough hook on a standing mixer, or your hands on a floured board, knead dough for 8 minutes. Dough should be smooth and elastic.

Place into a greased bowl and flip to cover all sides. Cover and allow to rise in a warm, dark place until doubled in size (about one hour).

GLUTEN-FREE | 2¼ CUPS GLUTEN-FREE FLOUR MIX | 2 tsp XANTHAN GUM

# PIE CRUST
YIELD: 3 9-INCH CRUSTS

**3 cups flour** (2½ cups whole wheat)
**2 teaspoons pink salt**
**1 teaspoon baking powder**
**1¼ cups shortening**
**1 tablespoon vinegar**
**1 cup water**

In a large bowl, mix flour, pink salt, and baking powder.

Using a pastry blender or your fingers, gently cut in shortening until just incorporated. Mixture should look crumbly with no large pieces of shortening. Add vinegar and water and mix with a wooden spoon or spatula until combined.

Divide into 3 equal sections.

Refrigerate sections that you aren't working with in an airtight container for up to one week.

GLUTEN-FREE | 3¾ CUPS GLUTEN-FREE FLOUR MIX | 4 tsp XANTHAN GUM

The secret to a flakey and tender crust is limited handling. Work the dough as little as possible.

# TORTILLAS
YIELD: 12 TORTILLAS

**2 cups flour** (1¾ cups whole wheat)
**½ teaspoon pink salt**
**1 teaspoon baking powder**
**1 teaspoon cumin**
**1 tablespoon fresh chopped oregano** (1 tsp dried oregano)
**1 tablespoon shortening**
**¾ cup water**

In a large mixing bowl, mix flour, pink salt, baking powder, cumin, and oregano.

Using your fingers, cut in shortening until incorporated. Add water and mix until incorporated.

Knead dough until smooth (about 2 minutes).

Preheat medium-sized skillet on medium-low heat (about 5 minutes).

Divide the dough into 12 equal pieces and roll into balls. On a floured board, flatten balls with the palm of your hand and, with a rolling pin, roll into paper-thin tortillas (about 8 inches in diameter).

Place each tortilla on the preheated pan and cook until golden brown on each side (about 1 minute per side).

Refrigerate in an airtight container for up to one week. Can be frozen for up to three months.

GLUTEN-FREE | 2½ CUPS GLUTEN-FREE FLOUR MIX | 1 tsp XANTHAN GUM

# PITA BREAD
YIELD: 8 PITAS

½ teaspoon yeast
1¼ cups warm water
3 cups flour (2½ cups whole wheat)
1 teaspoon pink salt
1 tablespoon grape seed oil

In a large mixing bowl, sprinkle yeast over warm water and stir to dissolve.

Add one cup of flour and stir for one minute. Cover and let rest for one hour.

Sprinkle pink salt over mixture. Add oil and mix well. Add remaining flour and mix until incorporated. Using the dough hook on a standing mixer, or your hands on a floured board, knead dough for 8 minutes. Dough should be smooth and elastic.

Place into a greased bowl and flip to cover all sides. Cover and allow to rise in a warm, dark place until doubled in size (about one hour).

Preheat oven to 450 degrees.

Punch dough and divide in half. Return the half that you are not working with to the greased bowl and cover.

Divide exposed dough into 4 equal sections. On a floured board, roll dough sections into 6-inch circles. Place onto parchment-lined baking sheets.

Bake in preheated oven until puffed and golden (3-4 minutes).

GLUTEN- FREE | 4 CUPS GLUTEN-FREE FLOUR MIX | 1 tsp XANTHAN GUM

# FRENCH BREAD
YIELD: 2-4 LOAVES

**2 cups warm water**
**1 package yeast**
**2 tablespoons sugar**
**1 tablespoon grape seed oil**
**1 tablespoon pink salt**
**5½ cups flour** (5 cups whole wheat)
**1 tablespoon water**

In a large mixing bowl, stir together yeast, warm water, and sugar. Let mixture sit for 10 minutes (should appear creamy).

Add oil, pink salt, and flour and mix until incorporated. Using the dough hook on a standing mixer, or your hands on a floured board, knead dough for 8 minutes. Dough should be smooth and elastic.

Place into a greased bowl and flip to cover all sides. Cover and allow to rise in a warm, dark place until doubled in size (about one hour).

Preheat oven to 375 degrees.

Punch dough and divide into two pieces (four if making medium loaves). Roll on a floured board until dough portions form 12-inch loaf shapes (6-inch for medium loaves).

Place onto a parchment-lined baking sheet, cover, and allow to rise for 30 minutes.

Bake in preheated oven for 20-25 minutes.

GLUTEN FREE | 5¾ CUPS GLUTEN-FREE FLOUR MIX | 1 tsp XANTHAN GUM

# YEAST ROLLS
YIELD: 12 ROLLS

1 package yeast
¼ cup warm water
¾ cup almond or rice milk
3 tablespoons shortening
3 tablespoons sugar
3 cups flour (2½ cups whole wheat)
1 teaspoon baking powder
1¼ teaspoons pink salt
1 teaspoon apple cider vinegar

In a small bowl, dissolve yeast in warm water.

In a small saucepan over medium-high heat, combine almond milk, shortening, and sugar. Stir until sugar is dissolved and shortening is melted. Cool to room temperature.

In a large mixing bowl, combine flour, baking powder, and pink salt. Add cooled almond milk mixture, yeast, and vinegar and mix until incorporated. Using the dough hook on a standing mixer, or your hands on a floured board, knead the dough for 8 minutes. Dough should be smooth and elastic.

Place into a greased bowl and flip to cover all sides. Cover and allow to rise in a warm, dark place until doubled in size (about one hour).

Preheat oven to 350 degrees.

Punch dough and divide into 12 equal pieces. Make an OK sign with your thumb and forefinger and press dough pieces through to create smooth balls, pinching and twisting the excess on the bottom to keep the dough taut.

Place side by side in a greased baking dish, cover, and allow to rise for 45 minutes.

Bake in preheated oven for 15-20 minutes until lightly golden on top.

GLUTEN-FREE | 4 CUPS GLUTEN-FREE FLOUR MIX | 1 tsp XANTHAN GUM

# GARLIC BREADSTICKS
YIELD: 12 LARGE OR 24 MINI BREADSTICKS

3 teaspoons yeast
¼ cup warm water
2½ cups flour (2 cups whole wheat)
½ teaspoon baking powder
1 tablespoon sugar
½ teaspoon pink salt
1 tablespoon minced garlic
2 tablespoons nutritional yeast
1 tablespoon chopped fresh basil (1 tsp dried basil)
1 tablespoon chopped fresh oregano (1 tsp dried oregano)
1 tablespoon shortening
¾ cup almond or rice milk
1 teaspoon apple cider vinegar
Shortening for brushing

In a small bowl, dissolve yeast in warm water.

In a large mixing bowl, mix flour, baking powder, sugar, pink salt, garlic, nutritional yeast, basil, and oregano.

Cut in shortening with fingers until combined.

Add dissolved yeast, almond milk, and vinegar and mix until incorporated. Using the dough hook on a standing mixer, or your hands on a floured board, knead dough for 8 minutes. Dough should be smooth and elastic.

Place into a greased bowl and flip to cover all sides. Cover and allow to rise in a warm, dark place until doubled in size (about one hour).

Punch dough and divide into 12 equal pieces (24 if making mini breadsticks). Roll dough pieces between your hands to create long, thin pieces. Holding dough at both ends, twist slightly.

Preheat oven to 375 degrees.

Place breadsticks onto a baking sheet, cover, and allow to rise for 30 minutes.

Bake in preheated oven for 10-15 minutes.

GLUTEN-FREE | 3 CUPS GLUTEN-FREE FLOUR MIX | ¾ tsp XANTHAN GUM

# CORNBREAD
YIELD: 12 SQUARES

2½ cups cornmeal
1½ cups flour (1¼ cups whole wheat)
2½ teaspoons baking powder
1½ teaspoons pink salt
½ cup sugar
2 cups almond or rice milk
3 tablespoons grape seed oil
1 tablespoon apple cider vinegar
1 cup chopped fresh corn (optional)

Preheat oven to 350 degrees.

Grease a 9x13-inch baking dish with shortening.

In a large bowl, mix cornmeal, flour, baking powder, pink salt, and sugar. Add almond milk, grape seed oil, vinegar, and corn and mix until incorporated.

Place the empty and greased baking dish in preheated oven for 10 minutes.

Remove and immediately pour in batter. Return to the oven for 25-30 minutes.

JALAPENO CORNBREAD
½ cup minced red onion
1 tablespoon minced jalapeno

Add minced onion and jalapeno with chopped fresh corn.

GLUTEN-FREE | 1½ CUPS GLUTEN-FREE FLOUR MIX | ½ tsp XANTHAN GUM

Heating the greased dish makes all the difference when making cornbread. This creates the crispy edges that separate the good from the great.

Strawberry Crepes (page 195)

# CREPES
YIELD: 12 CREPES

**2 tablespoons shortening, melted**
**1 cup flour** (1 cup whole wheat)
**1 tablespoon arrowroot powder**
**¼ teaspoon baking soda**
**⅛ teaspoon pink salt**
**¾ cup almond or rice milk**
**¾ cup water**

Melt shortening in a small saucepan over medium-high heat.

In a large bowl, combine flour, arrowroot, baking soda, and pink salt. Add almond milk, water, and shortening. Whisk until smooth.

Preheat skillet on medium-low heat for 5 minutes.

Pour ⅛ cup of batter onto the hot pan and tilt in all directions until it forms a 6-inch circle. Cook until batter bubbles (about 2 minutes). Carefully flip and cook an additional 2 minutes.

Refrigerate crepes in an airtight container for up to 1 week.

GLUTEN-FREE  |  1½ CUPS GLUTEN-FREE FLOUR MIX  |  ⅛ tsp XANTHAN GUM

# BISCUITS
YIELD: 12 BISCUITS

**2 cups flour** (1¾ cups whole wheat)
**¼ teaspoon baking soda**
**1 tablespoon baking powder**
**1 teaspoon pink salt**
**6 tablespoons shortening**
**1⅛ cups almond or rice milk**

Preheat oven to 350 degrees.

In a large mixing bowl, combine flour, baking soda, baking powder, and pink salt.

Using a pastry blender or your fingers, gently cut in the shortening until just combined. Mixture should appear crumbly with no large chunks of shortening.

Gently mix in almond milk with a spatula or wooden spoon until just incorporated.

Flip the dough onto a floured board and gently press with your palms until ¾-inch thick. Cut circles with biscuit or cookie cutter and place onto a baking sheet. Remold excess dough and continue to cut biscuits until all dough is used.

Bake in preheated oven until golden brown (about 12-15 minutes).

GLUTEN-FREE | 2½ CUPS GLUTEN-FREE FLOUR MIX | ¾ tsp XANTHAN GUM

The key to a great biscuit is in the dough. You want to handle and mix it as little as possible; literally mix until just incorporated. We don't even use a rolling pin. We just pat it out with our hands. Biscuits made with whole wheat flour will be more crumbly than those made with white.

# "CHEDDER" HERB BISCUITS
YIELD: 12 BISCUITS

**2 cups flour** (1¾ cups whole wheat)
**¼ teaspoon baking soda**
**1 tablespoon baking powder**
**1 teaspoon pink salt**
**2 tablespoons nutritional yeast**
**2 tablespoons chopped fresh chives** (1 tbsp dried chives)
**2 tablespoons chopped fresh parsley**
**¼ teaspoon cayenne pepper**
**6 tablespoons shortening**
**1¼ cups almond or rice milk**

Preheat oven to 350 degrees.

In a large mixing bowl, combine flour, baking soda, baking powder, pink salt, nutritional yeast, chives, parsley, and cayenne pepper.

Using a pastry blender or your fingers, gently cut in the shortening until just incorporated. Mixture should appear crumbly with no large chunks of shortening.

Gently mix in almond milk with a spatula or wooden spoon until just incorporated.

Flip the dough onto a floured board and gently press with your palms until ¾-inch thick. Cut circles with biscuit or cookie cutter and place onto a baking sheet. Remold excess dough and continue to cut biscuits until all dough is used.

Bake in preheated oven until golden brown (12-15 minutes).

---

GLUTEN-FREE | 2½ CUPS GLUTEN-FREE FLOUR MIX | ¾ tsp XANTHAN GUM

---

# ENGLISH MUFFINS
YIELD: 12 ENGLISH MUFFINS

1 teaspoon yeast
½ cup warm water
½ cup almond or rice milk
⅛ cup shortening
1 tablespoon sugar
2¾ cups flour (2½ cups whole wheat)
½ teaspoon pink salt
1 teaspoon baking soda

In a large mixing bowl, dissolve yeast in warm water. Cover and let sit for 10 minutes.

In a small saucepan over medium-high heat, combine almond milk, shortening, and sugar. Stir until sugar is dissolved and shortening melted. Cool to room temperature.

Combine 1½ cups of flour with the lukewarm almond milk mixture and yeast. Beat until smooth (about 2 minutes). Add pink salt, baking soda, and remaining flour, and mix until incorporated. Using the dough hook on a standing mixer, or your hands on a floured board, knead the dough for 8 minutes. Dough should be smooth and elastic.

Place into a greased bowl and flip to cover all sides. Cover and allow to rise in a warm, dark place until doubled in size (about one hour).

Punch the dough and divide in half. On a floured board, roll dough until ½-inch thick and cut into circles. Repeat with the other half.

Place onto parchment-lined baking sheets, cover, and let rise 30 minutes.

Preheat greased or nonstick, medium-sized skillet (with lid) on medium-low heat until hot (about 5 minutes). Place muffins onto the hot skillet and cook 5 minutes. Flip, cover, and cook an additional 5 minutes.

GLUTEN-FREE | 4 CUPS GLUTEN-FREE FLOUR MIX | 1 tsp XANTHAN GUM

# "BUTTER" CRACKERS
YIELD: 12 DOZEN

**2 cups flour** (1¾ cups whole wheat)
**1 tablespoon sugar**
**3 teaspoons baking powder**
**1 teaspoon pink salt**
**1 tablespoon apple cider vinegar**
**6 tablespoons shortening**
**⅔ cup water**
**shortening and pink salt**

Preheat oven to 400 degrees.

In a large mixing bowl, mix flour, sugar, baking powder, and pink salt.

Cut in shortening with your fingers.

Mix in water and vinegar until incorporated.

Divide dough in half.

Roll out half of the dough onto a floured board until paper thin, making sure thickness is consistent. Using a small circle cutter, cut out crackers and place onto a baking sheet until all dough is used.

Bake in preheated oven until golden brown (8-10 minutes).

While warm, brush with shortening and sprinkle with pink salt.

---

GLUTEN-FREE | 2½ CUPS GLUTEN-FREE FLOUR MIX | ½ tsp XANTHAN GUM

# SODA CRACKERS
YIELD: ABOUT 10 DOZEN

**2 cups flour** (1¾ cups whole wheat)
**1 teaspoon pink salt**
**½ teaspoon baking soda**
**2 tablespoons shortening**
**⅔ cup water**

Preheat oven to 375 degrees.

In a large bowl, mix flour, pink salt, and baking soda. Cut in shortening with your fingers until incorporated. Mix in water and knead until pliable (about one minute).

Divide the dough into 4 equal sections. On a floured board, roll each dough section until paper-thin. Sprinkle with pink salt and lightly roll to press salt into the dough. Using a pastry wheel, pizza cutter, or sharp knife, cut dough into 1½-inch squares.

Place onto a baking sheet and pierce twice with a fork, making 8 holes in each cracker.

Bake in preheated oven for 10-12 minutes.

GLUTEN-FREE | 2½ CUPS GLUTEN-FREE FLOUR MIX | ½ tsp XANTHAN GUM

# SAUCES and DRESSINGS

# FRESH HERB MARINARA
YIELD: 4 CUPS

I cup minced red onion
1 tablespoon minced garlic
⅛ cup grape seed oil
1 15 ounce can tomato sauce
1 15 ounce can diced tomatoes (or 2 cups chopped fresh tomatoes)
2 tablespoons chopped fresh basil (1 tbsp dried basil)
2 tablespoons chopped fresh oregano (1 tbsp dried oregano)
1 teaspoon chopped fresh thyme (½ tsp dried thyme)
½ teaspoon dried fennel
½ teaspoon dried marjoram
1 teaspoon pink salt

In a medium saucepan over medium-high heat, sauté onions and garlic in grape seed oil until onions are translucent (about 5 minutes).

Add tomato sauce, diced tomatoes, basil, oregano, thyme, fennel, marjoram, and pink salt.

Cover and simmer on low heat for 15 minutes.

Everyone loves pizza and spaghetti, and this is the best sauce in America. And in Italy. We hate calling for a canned food, but let's be honest, tomatoes are rarely in season. Make sure to always purchase organic.

# VODKA SAUCE
YIELD: 3 CUPS

I cup chopped red onion
1 tablespoon minced garlic
2 tablespoons grape seed oil
1 15 ounce can tomato sauce
1 cup almond or rice milk
2 tablespoons chopped fresh basil (1 tbsp dried basil)
1 tablespoon chopped parsley
1 teaspoon pink salt

In a medium-sized sauce pan over medium-high heat, sauté onion and garlic in grape seed oil until tender (about 5 minutes).

Add tomato sauce, almond milk, basil, parsley, and pink salt.

Reduce heat to low, cover, and simmer for 15 minutes.

# ENCHILADA SAUCE

YIELD: 3 CUPS

⅛ cup grape seed oil
¼ cup flour (¼ cup whole wheat)
2 cups Vegetable Stock
1 can tomato paste
1 tablespoon minced red onion
½ teaspoon minced garlic
1 tablespoon chopped fresh oregano (1 tsp dried oregano)
1 teaspoon cumin
½ teaspoon pink salt

In a medium saucepan over medium-high heat, mix grape seed oil and flour and stir until mixture bubbles.

Whisk in Vegetable Stock and tomato paste.

Stir in onion, garlic, oregano, cumin, and pink salt.

Cover and simmer on low heat for 20 minutes.

GLUTEN-FREE | 5 tbsp GLUTEN-FREE FLOUR MIX

# JERK SAUCE
YIELD: ABOUT 1 CUP

¼ cup coconut aminos (or tamari)
¼ cup ketchup
juice from 3 limes
½ cup brown sugar
¼ cup chopped fresh thyme
3 cloves garlic, minced
½ jalapeno, minced
2 tablespoons allspice
1 tablespoon nutmeg
1 teaspoon pink salt
1 cup chopped green onions

Place all ingredients (except green onions) into the container of a high-powered blender and puree.

Fold in green onions.

If you do not have a blender, whisk ingredients together until incorporated.

# TERIYAKI SAUCE
YIELD: 2 CUPS

1 cup coconut aminos (or tamari)
1¼ cups Vegetable Stock
½ cup brown sugar
1 teaspoon minced ginger
1 teaspoon minced garlic
¼ cup minced red onion

In a medium-sized bowl, combine all ingredients and whisk until incorporated.

# THAI PEANUT SAUCE
YIELD: 2 CUPS

1 clove garlic, minced
1 teaspoon minced ginger
⅛ cup grape seed oil
½ cup creamy, salted peanut butter
½ cup Vegetable Stock
1 tablespoon lime juice
3 tablespoons coconut aminos (or tamari)
½ jalapeno, minced
1 teaspoon crushed red pepper
2 green onions, chopped
⅛ cup chopped cilantro

In a medium saucepan over medium-high heat, lightly sauté garlic and ginger in grape seed oil for 2 minutes.

Whisk in peanut butter and Vegetable Stock until incorporated.

Add lime juice, coconut aminos, jalapeno, and crushed red pepper. Cover and simmer over low heat for 20 minutes.

Fold in green onions and cilantro.

# ASIAN SESAME SAUCE
YIELD: 2 CUPS

1½ cups Vegetable Stock
¼ cup apple cider vinegar
½ cup brown sugar
3 tablespoons coconut aminos (or tamari)
1 tablespoon Tahini
1½ teaspoons minced garlic
3 tablespoons arrowroot powder
½- 1 teaspoon crushed red pepper

In a medium saucepan over medium-high heat, combine all ingredients and whisk until incorporated.

Bring to a boil.

Reduce heat to low, cover, and simmer for 20 minutes.

# HOLLANDAISE SAUCE
YIELD: ABOUT 1 CUP

½ cup shortening
juice from 2 lemons
zest from 2 lemons
¼ cup almond or rice milk
1 tablespoon arrowroot powder
¼ teaspoon pink salt
¼ teaspoon black pepper

Place shortening, lemon juice, lemon zest, almond milk, arrowroot, and pink salt into the container of a high powered blender and process until smooth.

Fold in pepper.

Refrigerate in an airtight container for up to 1 week.

# BECHAMEL SAUCE
YIELD: 2 CUPS

¼ cup shortening
6 tablespoons flour (6 tbsp whole wheat)
2 cups almond or rice milk
4 tablespoons nutritional yeast
2 teaspoons pink salt
¼ teaspoon nutmeg

In a medium saucepan over medium-high heat, melt shortening. Mix in flour and stir until mixture bubbles. Whisk in almond milk and continue stirring until mixture thickens (about 2 minutes).

Remove from heat and add nutritional yeast, pink salt, and nutmeg.

GLUTEN-FREE | ½ cup GLUTEN-FREE FLOUR MIX

# RAW-VEGAN RANCH DRESSING
YIELD: 2 CUPS

**2 cups Cashew Cream**
**¼ cup water**
**½ teaspoon minced onion**
**¼ teaspoon minced garlic**
**1 teaspoon pink salt**
**¼ cup chopped dill**
**¼ cup chopped green onions or chives**
**¼ cup parsley**

Place Cashew Cream, water, onion, garlic, and pink salt into the container of a high-powered blender and process until smooth.

Fold in chopped herbs.

Refrigerate in an airtight container for up to 5 days.

# ITALIAN DRESSING
YIELD: ABOUT 2 CUPS

1 cup grape seed oil
½ cup apple cider vinegar
1 clove garlic, minced
1 tablespoon minced red onion
½ teaspoon Tahini
1 rib celery, minced
¼ cup chopped parsley
2 tablespoons minced fresh basil (1 tbsp dried basil)
1 tablespoon minced fresh oregano (1 tsp dried oregano)
1 teaspoon pink salt

In a medium-sized bowl, whisk together all ingredients.

Refrigerate in an airtight container for up to 1 week.

# BALSAMIC VINAIGRETTE
YIELD: 1 ½ CUPS

¾ cup grape seed oil
¼ cup balsamic vinegar
1 clove garlic, minced
1 tablespoon dijon mustard
1 teaspoon agave nectar
½ teaspoon pink salt
½ teaspoon black pepper

In a medium-sized bowl, whisk together all ingredients.

Refrigerate in an airtight container for up to 1 week.

# CITRUS VINAIGRETTE
YIELD: 1 CUP

½ cup orange juice
2 tablespoons lemon juice
2 tablespoons lime juice
2 tablespoons grape seed oil
1 tablespoon agave nectar
1 tablespoon dijon mustard
1 tablespoon coconut aminos (or tamari)
1 tablespoon minced ginger

In a medium-sized bowl, whisk together all ingredients.

Refrigerate in an airtight container for up to 1 week.

# SOUPS and DIPS

# SEA VEGETABLE CHOWDER
YIELD: 4 CUPS

⅛ cup wakame
1½ cups cubed sweet potatoes
⅛ cup grape seed oil
½ cup minced red onion
1 clove garlic, minced
½ cup chopped celery
1 cup diced mushrooms
½ cup diced carrots
3 tablespoons shortening
¼ cup flour (¼ cup whole wheat)
2 cups almond or rice milk
1 cup Vegetable Stock
2 tablespoons nutritional yeast
1 teaspoon pink salt
½ teaspoon black pepper

Rinse wakame. In a small bowl, cover with water and soak for 15 minutes. Rinse again.

In a medium saucepan over medium-high heat, boil cubed sweet potatoes until just tender (about 20 minutes).

In a large skillet over medium-high heat, sauté onions, garlic, and celery in grape seed oil until onions are translucent (about 5 minutes). Add mushrooms, cooked sweet potatoes, and carrots and sauté an additional 5 minutes.

In a large saucepan over medium-high heat, melt shortening. Stir in flour and continue to cook until small bubbles form. Whisk in almond milk and continue stirring until mixture thickens (about 2 minutes). Whisk in Vegetable Stock and nutritional yeast.

Add wakame, sauteed vegetables, pink salt, and pepper.

Reduce heat to low, cover, and simmer for 20 minutes.

Serve with Soda Crackers (page 65).

GLUTEN-FREE | 5 tbsp GLUTEN-FREE FLOUR MIX

# "CREAM" OF BROCCOLI SOUP
YIELD: 4 CUPS

¼ cup grape seed oil
1½ cups minced red onion
1 stalk celery, chopped
4 cups chopped broccoli
1½ cups Vegetable Stock
2 tablespoons shortening
3 tablespoons flour (3 tbsp whole wheat)
1 cup almond or rice milk
¼ cup chopped parsley
1 teaspoon pink salt
1 teaspoon black pepper

In a large saucepan over medium-high heat, sauté onion and celery in grape seed oil until translucent (about 5 minutes).

Add broccoli and Vegetable Stock. Reduce heat to low, cover, and simmer for 10 minutes.

In a medium saucepan over medium-high heat, melt shortening. Stir in flour and continue to cook until small bubbles form. Whisk in almond milk and continue to cook until mixture thickens (about 2 minutes).

Add almond milk mixture, parsley, pink salt, and pepper to broccoli mixture.

Reduce heat to low, cover, and simmer for 20 minutes.

GLUTEN-FREE | 4 tbsp GLUTEN-FREE FLOUR MIX

# TOMATO BASIL SOUP
YIELD: 4 CUPS

⅛ cup grape seed oil
1 small red onion, minced
1 clove garlic, minced
1 can diced tomatoes
1 cup Vegetable Stock
½ cup chopped fresh basil
1 cup almond or rice milk
1 teaspoon pink salt
1 teaspoon black pepper

In a large saucepan over medium-high heat, sauté onions and garlic in grape seed oil until tender (about 5 minutes).

Add diced tomatoes, Vegetable Stock, and basil.

Reduce heat to low, cover, and simmer for 10 minutes.

Add almond milk, pink salt, and pepper.

Transfer to the container of a high-powdered blender and puree in batches.

Return to the saucepan.

Simmer over low heat for 10 minutes.

# RED LENTIL SOUP
YIELD: 8 CUPS

**2 tablespoons grape seed oil**
**1 small red onion, chopped**
**1 clove garlic, minced**
**2 ribs celery, chopped**
**4 medium carrots, chopped**
**1 can diced tomatoes**
**2 cups Vegetable Stock**
**2 cups water**
**1 teaspoon cumin**
**1 teaspoon pink salt**
**1 cup red lentils**
**3 cups chopped kale**
**1 teaspoon black pepper**

In a large soup pot over medium-high heat, sauté onions, garlic, celery, and carrots in grape seed oil until tender (about 8 minutes).

Add diced tomatoes, Vegetable Stock, water, cumin, and pink salt.

Bring to a boil.

Add lentils. Reduce heat to low, cover, and simmer until lentils are cooked (about 10 minutes).

Remove from heat and stir in kale and pepper.

# VEGETABLE SOUP
YIELD: 8 CUPS

1 small eggplant, cubed
¾ cup grape seed oil
3 teaspoons chopped fresh thyme
4 cloves garlic, minced
1 medium red onion, chopped
2 ribs celery, chopped
2 carrots, chopped
2 cups chopped green beans
2 cups cubed sweet potatoes
2 cans diced tomatoes
2 cups Vegetable Stock
1 tablespoon coconut aminos (or tamari)
1 teaspoon pink salt
1 teaspoon black pepper

In a small bowl, cover cubed eggplant with ½ cup grape seed oil, chopped thyme, and one clove minced garlic. Massage with your hands to make sure all pieces are covered. Marinate for at least 30 minutes.

In a large soup pot over medium-high heat, sauté remaining garlic, onion, celery, carrots, green beans, and sweet potatoes in remaining grape seed oil until tender (about 8 minutes).

Add eggplant and cook an additional 2 minutes.

Add tomatoes, Vegetable Stock, and coconut aminos.

Bring to a boil.

Reduce heat to low, cover, and simmer for 30 minutes.

# FOUR BEAN CHILI
YIELD: ABOUT 12 CUPS

⅛ cup grape seed oil
1 medium onion, chopped
2 cloves garlic, minced
1 small green pepper, chopped
1 can tomato sauce
1 can diced tomatoes
1 cup Vegetable Stock
2 cups cooked black beans
1½ cups cooked kidney beans
1½ cups cooked pinto beans
1½ cups white beans
1 teaspoon sugar
1 tablespoon apple cider vinegar
1 tablespoon cumin
2 tablespoons chopped fresh oregano (1 tbsp dried oregano)
1 teaspoon chili powder
1 teaspoon pink salt

In a large soup pot over medium-high heat, sauté onions, garlic, and green peppers in grape seed oil until tender (about 5 minutes).

Add tomato sauce, diced tomatoes, Vegetable Stock, beans, sugar, vinegar, cumin, oregano, chili powder, and pink salt.

Reduce heat to low, cover, and simmer for 20 minutes.

Serve with Cashew Cream (page 43) and shredded Firm "Cheese" (page 36).

# MINESTONE SOUP
YIELD: ABOUT 12 CUPS

3 tablespoons grape seed oil
1 small red onion, chopped
3 cloves garlic, minced
1 rib celery, chopped
1 medium carrot, chopped
1 cup chopped green beans
1 can diced tomatoes
4 cups Vegetable Stock
3 cups water
2 cups cooked kidney beans
2 cups cooked white beans
2 tablespoons chopped fresh basil (1 tbsp dried basil)
2 tablespoons chopped fresh oregano (1 tbsp dried oregano)
1 teaspoon chopped fresh thyme (½ tsp dried thyme)
1 tablespoon minced parsley
½ cup brown rice pasta shells
2 teaspoons pink salt
3 cups chopped kale
½ teaspoon black pepper

In a large soup pot over medium-high heat, sauté onions, garlic, celery, carrots, and green beans in grape seed oil until tender (about 8 minutes).

Add diced tomatoes, Vegetable Stock, water, cooked beans, basil, oregano, thyme, and parsley.

Bring to a boil.

Reduce heat to low. Add pasta, pink salt, and pepper.

Cover and simmer for 20 minutes.

Stir in chopped kale and black pepper.

Serve with Garlic Breadsticks (page 56)

# CREOLE GUMBO

YIELD: 8 CUPS

¼ cup wakame
¼ cup grape seed oil
1 medium red onion, chopped
4 cloves garlic, minced
2 stalks celery, chopped
2 cups chopped okra
1½ cups chopped mushrooms
½ green pepper, chopped
½ jalapeno, minced
1½ cups chopped zucchini
⅛ cup shortening
3 tablespoons flour (3 tbsp whole wheat)
4 cups Vegetable Stock
2 cans diced tomatoes
⅛ cup sugar
⅛ cup coconut aminos (or tamari)
2 tablespoons chopped fresh thyme
2 bay leaves
1 teaspoon pink salt
1 teaspoon black pepper
chopped "Sausage" (optional)

Rinse wakame. In a small bowl, cover with water and soak for 15 minutes. Rinse again.

In a large saucepan over medium-high heat, sauté onion, garlic, celery, okra, mushrooms, green pepper, jalapeno, and zucchini in grape seed oil until tender (about 8 minutes).

In a large soup pot over medium-high heat, melt shortening. Mix in flour and continue to cook until mixture starts to bubble. Whisk in Vegetable Stock and continue to cook until mixture thickens (about 2 minutes). Add tomatoes, water, sugar, coconut aminos, thyme, bay leaves, and vegetable mixture.

Bring to a boil.

Reduce heat to low. Add wakame, cover, and simmer for one hour.

Remove bay leaves. Add pink salt, pepper, and chopped "Sausage."

# SWEET POTATO PECAN SOUP
YIELD: 8 CUPS

**2 medium sweet potatoes**
**⅛ cup grape seed oil**
**⅛ cup shortening**
**1 cup chopped red onion**
**1 medium-sized leek, chopped** (white and pale green portions)
**1 clove garlic, minced**
**5 cups Vegetable Stock**
**1 teaspoon pink salt**
**1 cinnamon stick**
**¼ teaspoon nutmeg**
**Candied Pecans**

Preheat oven to 425 degrees.

Cut sweet potatoes into ¼ inch slices. Cover in grape seed oil, place in a foil-lined baking dish, and roast in preheated oven until soft (about 30 minutes).

In a large soup pot over medium-high heat, melt shortening and sauté onions, chopped leek, and garlic until tender (about 5 minutes).

Add sweet potatoes, Vegetable Stock, cinnamon stick, and nutmeg. Bring to a boil.

Reduce heat to low, cover, and simmer for 20 minutes. Remove cinnamon stick.

Puree in batches in a high-powered blender.

Return to the soup pot and add pink salt.

Garnish with Candied Pecans.

---

CANDIED PECANS
**¼ cup shortening, melted**
**1 pound pecan halves**
**1 cup sugar**
**¾ teaspoon pink salt**
**½ teaspoon cinnamon**

Preheat oven to 250 degrees.

In a small bowl, combine sugar, pink salt, and cinnamon. Toss pecans in melted shortening until all are coated. Then toss in the sugar mixture and place onto a parchment-lined baking sheet.

Bake in preheated oven for one hour, tossing every 15 minutes.

# KALE ARTICHOKE DIP
YIELD: 4 CUPS

1 large artichoke
3 tablespoons shortening
¼ cup flour (¼ cup whole wheat)
1½ cups almond or rice milk
1⅛ cups nutritional yeast
½ cup minced onion
1 teaspoon minced garlic
2 cups chopped kale
½ teaspoon crushed red pepper
½ teaspoon pink salt
1 teaspoon black pepper

Preheat oven to 375 degrees.

STEAM ARTICHOKE
Using a sharp knife, cut off the top inch of the artichoke. Remove the stem and tough bottom leaves.

Boil 3 inches of water in a large saucepan. Place prepared artichoke bottom-side down into the water, cover, and steam for 30 minutes.

Remove the artichoke and allow it to cool enough to handle (about 10 minutes). Remove the leaves and scrape the bottom of each with a spoon to obtain the tender "meat." Continue until all leaves are removed.

Spoon out the choke (prickly and inedible portion). Coarsely chop the remaining artichoke heart and combine with the "meat" that you scraped from the leaves.

In a large saucepan over medium heat, melt shortening. Mix in flour and continue to cook until small bubbles form. Whisk in almond milk and cook until mixture thickens (about 2 minutes).

Stir in 1 cup of nutritional yeast.

In a large bowl, combine almond milk mixture, artichoke "meat," onion, garlic, kale, crushed red pepper, pink salt, and pepper.

Place mixture into a quart-sized baking dish and sprinkle with remaining nutritional yeast.

Bake in preheated oven for 15-20 minutes.

GLUTEN-FREE | 5 tbsp GLUTEN-FREE FLOUR MIX

# HUMMUS
YIELD: 4 CUPS

**4 cups cooked chickpeas**
**4 garlic cloves, minced**
**⅔ cup Tahini**
**¼ cup grape seed oil**
**2 cups water**
**juice from 2 lemons**
**2 teaspoons pink salt**

In a food processor (with S blade) or blender, puree all ingredients until smooth.

Refrigerate in an airtight container for up to 1 week.

# BABA GHANOUSH
YIELD: ABOUT 2 CUPS

**2 cups Pureed Eggplant**
**¼ cup lemon juice**
**¼ cup Tahini**
**1 clove garlic, minced**
**1½ tablespoons grape seed oil**
**1 teaspoon pink salt**
**½ teaspoon black pepper**

In a food processor (with S blade) or blender, puree all ingredients until smooth.

# RAW-VEGAN TZATZIKI
YIELD: ABOUT 2 CUPS

**2 cups Cashew Cream**
**½ large cucumber, skinned and seeds removed**
**1 teaspoon minced garlic**
**2 tablespoons lemon juice**
**3 tablespoons chopped, fresh dill**
**1 teaspoon pink salt**
**1 teaspoon black pepper**

Place Cashews Cream, cucumber, garlic, lemon juice, and pink salt into the container of a high-powered blender.

Blend until smooth.

Stir in dill and black pepper.

# PICO DE GALLO
YIELD: ABOUT 2 CUPS

**2 medium tomatoes, chopped**
**¼ cup minced red onion**
**¼ teaspoon minced garlic**
**Juice from ½ lime**
**2 tablespoons chopped cilantro** (optional)
**½ teaspoon pink salt**

Combine all ingredients in a medium-sized bowl.

# GUACAMOLE
YIELD: ABOUT 2 CUPS

**2 ripe, medium-sized avocados**
**½ cup chopped tomatoes**
**2 tablespoons minced red onion**
**Juice from ½ lime**
**1 teaspoon pink salt**

In a medium-sized bowl, mash avocados with the back of a fork.

Fold in remaining ingredients.

Serve immediately.

# MEXICAN BEAN DIP
YIELD: SERVES 8

**4 cups Refried Black Beans** (page 172)
**2 cups Soft "Cheese"**
**2 cups Guacamole** (page 97)
**2 cups Pico de Gallo** (page 97)
**2 cups chopped kale**
**1 cup Cashew Cream**
**½ cup grated Firm "Cheese"**

Cover the bottom of a 9x13-inch baking dish with the Refried Black Beans.

Cover beans with the Soft "Cheese."

Spread the Guacamole over the Soft "Cheese."

Cover with the chopped kale. Then with the Pico de Gallo.

Drizzle Cashew Cream over the dip, then sprinkle with grated Firm "Cheese."

Serve with vegan tortilla chips.

# CARAMELIZED ONION DIP
YIELD: 2 CUPS

3 tablespoons grape seed oil
4 cups coarsely chopped yellow onion
1 tablespoon brown sugar
2 tablespoons balsamic vinegar
½ teaspoon pink salt
1 teaspoon black pepper
⅛ cup shortening
⅛ cup flour (⅛ cup whole wheat)
2 tablespoons arrowroot
1½ cups almond or rice milk
¼ cup nutritional yeast
½ teaspoon coconut aminos (or tamari)
½ teaspoon minced garlic

CARAMELIZE ONIONS
In a large saucepan over medium-high heat, sauté onions in grape seed oil until translucent (about 10 minutes).

Stir in brown sugar, balsamic vinegar, ½ teaspoon pink salt, and ½ teaspoon black pepper

Reduce heat to low and simmer for 30 minutes, stirring occasionally.

In a large saucepan over medium-high heat, melt shortening. Mix in flour and arrowroot and stir until small bubbles form. Whisk in almond milk and continue to cook until mixture thickens (about 2 minutes).

Remove from the heat and stir in nutritional yeast, coconut aminos, and minced garlic.

In a large bowl, combine almond milk mixture, caramelized onions, and ½ teaspoon black pepper.

GLUTEN-FREE | 3 tbsp GLUTEN-FREE FLOUR MIX

# PIMENTO "CHEESE"
YIELD: ABOUT 2 CUPS

**1 medium red pepper** (or ½ cup pimentos)
**1 cup Soft "Cheese"**
**½ cup grated Firm "Cheese"**
**¼ teaspoon pink salt**

---

ROAST PEPPER

Preheat oven to 450 degrees.

Place red pepper on a baking sheet lined with foil. Roast for 30 minutes, turning pepper with tongs after 15 minutes.

Remove and immediately wrap roasted pepper in foil. Let sit for 30 minutes.

Cut cooled pepper into quarters, remove skin, and dice.

Save juices from the bottom of the foil.

---

In a large bowl, combine Soft "Cheese," grated Firm "Cheese," diced roasted red pepper, pink salt, and roasting juices.

# SEA VEGETABLE DIP
YIELD: 4 CUPS

¼ cup wakame
2 tablespoons grape seed oil
2 ribs celery, chopped
1 teaspoon minced garlic
2 tablespoons minced red onion
3 tablespoons shortening
¼ cup flour (¼ cup whole wheat)
1½ cups almond or rice milk
¾ cup nutritional yeast
1 teaspoon baking powder
1 teaspoon apple cider vinegar
½ teaspoon minced ginger
¼ teaspoon allspice
⅛ teaspoon nutmeg
pinch ground cloves
1 teaspoon dijon mustard
1 teaspoon pink salt
1 teaspoon black pepper
2 green onions chopped
½ cup chopped parsley
2 cups chopped kale
¼ teaspoon crushed red pepper

Rinse wakame. In a small bowl, cover with water and soak for 15 minutes. Rinse again.

In a skillet over medium-high heat, sauté celery, garlic, and onions in grape seed oil until tender (about 5 minutes).

In a large saucepan over medium-high heat, melt shortening. Mix in flour and continue to cook until small bubbles form. Whisk in almond milk and continue to cook until mixture thickens (about 2 minutes). Remove from heat and stir in nutritional yeast.

In a large bowl, combine almond milk mixture, wakame, baking powder, vinegar, ginger, allspice, nutmeg, cloves, mustard, salt and pepper. Fold in green onions, parsley, kale, and crushed red pepper.

Serve with "Butter" Crackers (page 63)

GLUTEN FREE | 5 tbsp GLUTEN-FREE FLOUR MIX

# MUSHROOM DIP
YIELD: ABOUT 2 CUPS

1 cup chopped Portobello mushrooms
2 cloves garlic, minced
⅛ cup grape seed oil
3 tablespoons shortening
¼ cup flour (¼ cup whole wheat)
1 cup almond or rice milk
1 cup nutritional yeast
2 cups chopped kale
½ teaspoon pink salt
¼ teaspoon black pepper

In a skillet over medium-high heat, sauté garlic and mushrooms until cooked through (about 5 minutes).

In a large saucepan over medium-high heat, melt shortening. Add flour and continue to cook until small bubbles form. Whisk in almond milk and cook until mixture thickens (about 2 minutes).

Remove from heat and stir in nutritional yeast.

Fold in mushroom mixture, kale, pink salt, and pepper.

Serve warm with thinly sliced French Bread (page 54).

GLUTEN-FREE | 5 tbsp GLUTEN-FREE FLOUR MIX

# BREAKFAST
# and
# LUNCH

# GLAZED DOUGHNUTS
YIELD: 12 DOUGHNUTS

1 package yeast
3 tablespoons warm water
6 tablespoons almond or rice milk
1 teaspoon apple cider vinegar
1½ tablespoons shortening
½ teaspoon pink salt
¼ cup sugar
1 teaspoon baking powder
2¼ cups flour (2 cups whole wheat)
GLAZE
2½ tablespoons shortening
1 cup powdered sugar
1½ teaspoons vanilla
2-3 tablespoons almond or rice milk

In a large mixing bowl, mix yeast and warm water and let sit for 10 minutes.

Add almond milk, vinegar, shortening, pink salt, sugar, baking powder, and 1 cup of flour. Beat on medium speed for 2 minutes. Then add remaining flour ½ cup at a time.

Using the dough hook on a standing mixer, or your hands on a floured board, knead dough for 8 minutes. Dough should be smooth and elastic. Place in a greased bowl and flip to cover all sides. Cover and allow to rise in a warm, dark place until doubled in size (about one hour).

Punch the dough. Separate into 12 equal pieces. Roll each piece into a smooth ball, then flatten with your palms. Poke a hole into the middle of the dough disc and shape into a doughnut.

Place each doughnut onto a parchment-lined baking sheet and allow to rise an additional 30 minutes. If you are making doughnuts for the next morning, cover and refrigerate.

MAKE GLAZE
In a small saucepan, heat shortening until melted. Add almond milk and vanilla. Whisk in powdered sugar.

In a large saucepan, heat 2 inches of grape seed oil on medium heat. The ideal temperature is 350 degrees and a candy thermometer will ensure consistent results. Place each doughnut into hot oil for 1 minute on each side. Place on a paper towel-lined baking sheet to absorb excess oil. Cover with glaze.

GLUTEN-FREE | 2½ CUPS GLUTEN-FREE FLOUR MIX | 1 tsp XANTHAN GUM

# WAFFLES
YIELD: ABOUT 12 WAFFLES

1¼ cups flour (1 cup whole wheat)
2 tablespoons arrowroot powder
2 teaspoons baking powder
½ teaspoon baking soda
½ teaspoon pink salt
½ cup grape seed oil
1¼ cups almond or rice milk
2 teaspoons apple cider vinegar

In a medium-sized mixing bowl, combine flour, arrowroot, baking powder, baking soda, and pink salt.

Whisk in grape seed oil, almond milk, and vinegar.

Cook according to waffle maker's directions.

Refrigerate leftover batter in an airtight container for up to one week.

GLUTEN-FREE | 1½ CUPS GLUTEN-FREE FLOUR MIX | ½ tsp XANTHAN GUM

# PANCAKES
YIELD: 2 CUPS BATTER

**I cup flour** (1 cup whole wheat)
**2 teaspoons baking powder**
**½ teaspoon pink salt**
**1¾ cups almond or rice milk**
**3 tablespoons grape seed oil**
**1 teaspoon apple cider vinegar**

Preheat skillet or griddle to medium-high heat.

In a medium-sized bowl, combine flour, baking powder, and pink salt.

Whisk in almond milk, grape seed oil, and vinegar.

Pour batter in desired shapes onto preheated skillet or griddle.

Wait for batter to bubble, then flip. Continue cooking 1-2 minutes until pancake is cooked through.

Refrigerate leftover batter in an airtight container for up to 1 week.

BLUEBERRY PANCAKES: Add ½ cup blueberries and ½ teaspoon vanilla

CHOCOLATE CHIP PANCAKES: Add ½ cup chocolate chips and ½ teaspoon vanilla

GLUTEN-FREE | 1½ CUPS GLUTEN-FREE FLOUR MIX | ⅛ tsp XANTHAN GUM

# CHOCOLATE CHIP MUFFINS
YIELD: 12 MUFFINS

**2 cups flour** (1¾ cups whole wheat)
**½ cup sugar**
**3 teaspoons baking powder**
**½ teaspoon pink salt**
**1 cup almond or rice milk**
**⅓ cup grape seed oil**
**1 teaspoon apple cider vinegar**
**1 teaspoon vanilla**
**¾ cup chocolate chips**

Preheat oven to 400 degrees.

Grease and flour muffin tins or line with baking cups.

In a large mixing bowl, combine flour, sugar, baking powder, and pink salt.

Mix in almond milk, grape seed oil, vinegar, and vanilla.

Fold in chocolate chips.

Fill muffin cups ⅔ full.

Bake in preheated oven for 20-25 minutes (inserted toothpick should come out clean).

Cool in pan for 5 minutes.

GLUTEN-FREE | 2¼ CUPS GLUTEN-FREE FLOUR MIX | ¾ tsp XANTHAN GUM

# BANANA NUT MUFFINS
YIELD: 12 MUFFINS

1¼ cups flour (1 cup whole wheat)
¾ teaspoon baking powder
½ teaspoon baking soda
¼ teaspoon pink salt
¾ cup sugar
3 tablespoons almond or rice milk
1 teaspoon apple cider vinegar
1 tablespoon vanilla
1½ very ripe bananas
¾ cup chopped walnuts

Preheat oven to 400 degrees.

Grease and flour muffin tins or line with baking cups.

In a large mixing bowl, combine flour, baking powder, baking soda, pink salt, and sugar.

Mix in almond milk, vinegar, and vanilla.

Gently break up bananas with your hands and incorporate into batter.

Fold in walnuts.

Fill muffin cups ⅔ full.

Bake in preheated oven for 20 minutes (inserted toothpick should come out clean).

Cool in pan for 5 minutes.

GLUTEN-FREE | 1½ CUPS GLUTEN-FREE FLOUR MIX | ½ tsp XANTHAN GUM

# BLUEBERRY MUFFINS
YIELD: 12 MUFFINS

**1½ cups flour** (1¼ cups whole wheat)
**¾ cup sugar**
**½ teaspoon pink salt**
**2 teaspoons baking powder**
**⅓ cup grape seed oil**
**⅔ cup almond or rice milk**
**1 teaspoon apple cider vinegar**
**1 teaspoon vanilla**
**1 cup blueberries**
**CRUMB TOPPING**
**⅛ cup shortening**
**¼ cup sugar**
**¼ cup flour** (¼ cup whole wheat)
**1½ teaspoons cinnamon**

Preheat oven to 400 degrees.

Grease and flour muffin tins or line with baking cups.

---

MAKE CRUMB TOPPING
In a small bowl, combine shortening, sugar, flour, and cinnamon. Mixture should be crumbly. Set aside.

---

In a large mixing bowl, combine flour, sugar, pink salt, and baking powder.

Add grape seed oil, almond milk, vinegar, and vanilla and mix until incorporated.

Fold in blueberries.

Fill muffin cups ⅔ full and cover with crumb topping.

Bake in preheated oven for 20 minutes (inserted toothpick should come out clean).

Cool in pan for 5 minutes.

---

GLUTEN-FREE | 1¾ CUPS GLUTEN-FREE FLOUR MIX | ½ tsp XANTHAN GUM
5 tbsp GLUTEN-FREE FLOUR MIX

---

# CINNAMON ROLLS
YIELD: 12 CINNAMON ROLLS

1 cup almond or rice milk
1 teaspoon apple cider vinegar
⅓ cup shortening
4 cups flour (3½ cups whole wheat)
1 teaspoon baking powder
1 teaspoon pink salt
2½ teaspoons yeast

---

MAKE DOUGH

In a medium saucepan over medium heat, melt shortening in almond milk.

In a large mixing bowl, combine flour, yeast, baking powder, and pink salt. Mix in almond milk mixture and vinegar until combined.

Using the dough hook on a standing mixer, or your hands on a floured board, knead dough for 8 minutes. Dough should be smooth and elastic.

Place dough into a greased bowl and rotate so that all sides are covered. Cover and allow to rise for one hour.

---

GLUTEN-FREE | 4½ CUPS GLUTEN-FREE FLOUR MIX | 2 tsp XANTHAN GUM

**1 cup brown sugar**
**2½ teaspoons cinnamon**
**⅓ cup shortening**

MAKE FILLING
In a small bowl, combine brown sugar and cinnamon. Reserve shortening.

**¼ cup shortening**
**1½ cups powdered sugar**
**1 tablespoon nutritional yeast**
**1 teaspoon vanilla**
**⅛ teaspoon pink salt**
**⅛ cup almond milk**

MAKE ICING
In a small saucepan over medium heat, melt shortening.

Remove from heat and stir in powdered sugar and nutritional yeast. Whisk in almond milk and vanilla.

Preheat oven to 400 degrees.

Grease a 9x13-inch baking dish.

Punch the dough.

On a floured board, roll the dough into a 16x21-inch rectangle.

Spread ⅓ cup shortening over flattened dough. Sprinkle with prepared filling. Starting at the 21-inch side, tightly roll dough, creating a long, thick cylinder.

Cut rolled dough into 12 equal pieces.

Place each roll into the greased baking dish, side-by-side. Cover dish and allow to rise for an additional 30 minutes.

Bake in preheated oven for 15 minutes.

Immediately cover with icing.

# BLUEBERRY SCONES
YIELD: 12 SCONES

**2 cups flour** (1¾ cups whole wheat)
**¼ cup brown sugar**
**1 tablespoon baking powder**
**¼ teaspoon pink salt**
**¼ cup shortening**
**1 cup blueberries**
**¾ cup almond or rice milk**
**1 tablespoon apple cider vinegar**
**LEMON GLAZE**
**1 teaspoon shortening, melted**
**1½ cups powdered sugar**
**zest and juice from 1 lemon**

Preheat oven to 350 degrees.

In a large bowl, mix flour, brown sugar, and pink salt.

Using pastry blender or your fingers, cut in shortening until just incorporated. Gently fold in blueberries. Stir in almond milk and vinegar until just incorporated.

Flip the dough onto a floured board. Sprinkle flour over the top of the dough, and using your hands, pat into a rectangle about ½-inch thick.

Using a sharp knife, cut the dough into thirds down the length, then in half perpendicularly making 6 squares. Cut each square diagonally, making 12 triangular scones. The dough will be very sticky and you may have to wipe the blade after each cut.

Do not get discouraged: the scones do not have to be perfect and can be reshaped on the baking sheet.

Place scones onto a parchment-lined baking sheet.

Bake in preheated oven for 10-15 minutes until slightly browned.

MAKE GLAZE
Melt shortening in a small saucepan over medium heat. In a medium-sized bowl, whisk melted shortening, sugar, and lemon juice until smooth

Cover scones with glaze while they're warm.

GLUTEN-FREE | 2½ CUPS GLUTEN-FREE FLOUR MIX | ¾ tsp XANTHAN GUM

# FIG BREAKFAST COOKIES
YIELD: 18 COOKIES

1½ cups flour (1¼ cup whole wheat)
½ cup rolled oats
¾ cup brown sugar
2 teaspoons baking powder
½ teaspoon baking soda
½ teaspoon cinnamon
¼ teaspoon allspice
¼ teaspoon pink salt
¼ cup grape seed oil
½ cup almond or rice milk
2 teaspoons apple cider vinegar
1 teaspoon vanilla
½ cup chopped dried figs
¼ cup chopped walnuts

Preheat oven to 375 degrees.

In a large bowl, mix flour, oats, brown sugar, baking powder, baking soda, cinnamon, allspice, and pink salt.

Create a well in the dry ingredient mixture. Add grape seed oil, almond milk, vinegar, and vanilla. Mix until incorporated.

Fold in figs and walnuts.

Spoon ⅛ cup portions of batter onto a parchment-lined baking sheet.

Bake in preheated oven for 10-15 minutes.

GLUTEN-FREE | 1¾ CUPS GLUTEN-FREE FLOUR MIX | ½ tsp XANTHAN GUM

# BERRY PARFAITS

YIELD: 4 PARFAITS

2 cups "Custard"
2 ripe bananas, sliced
1 cup strawberries, chopped
1 cup blueberries
1 cup chopped walnuts

You will need four 16-ounce glasses.

Begin by spooning ⅛ cup "Custard" into the bottom of each glass. Then layer ¼ banana (sliced) over "Custard." Sprinkle ⅛ cup chopped walnuts over banana slices. Spoon ⅛ cup "Custard" over nuts. Add ¼ cup strawberries and ¼ cup blueberries. Spoon ⅛ cup of "Custard" over berries. Layer ¼ banana followed by ⅛ cup chopped walnuts.

Finish each parfait by spooning ⅛ cup "Custard" on top.

# BANANA QUINOA OATMEAL

YIELD: SERVES 4

1¼ cups water
1¼ cups almond or rice milk
⅛ cup quinoa
4 cups rolled oats
½ teaspoon cinnamon
¼ teaspoon pink salt
2 ripe bananas, chopped
¼ cup brown sugar
1 teaspoon vanilla
¼ cup chopped walnuts

In a medium saucepan over medium-high heat, combine water, almond milk, and quinoa. Bring to a boil.

Reduce heat to low, cover, and simmer for five minutes.

Stir in oats, cinnamon, and pink salt.

Cover and simmer for an additional 5 minutes (until mixture thickens).

Remove from heat. Fold in bananas, brown sugar, vanilla, and walnuts.

# "SAUSAGE" KALE FRITTATA
YIELD: 1 9-INCH FRITTATA

**6 tablespoons shortening**
**½ cup flour** (½ cup whole wheat)
**2 tablespoons arrowroot powder**
**2 cups almond or rice milk**
**¼ cup nutritional yeast**
**3 teaspoons baking powder**
**3 teaspoons apple cider vinegar**
**½ cup minced red onion**
**1 clove garlic, minced**
**1 teaspoon pink salt**
**1 teaspoon black pepper**
**½ cup shredded Firm "Cheese"**
**2 cups chopped kale**
**3 "Sausage" patties chopped**

Preheat oven to 375 degrees.

Grease a 9-inch pie pan.

In a medium saucepan over medium-high heat, melt shortening. Mix in flour and cook until small bubbles form. Whisk in almond milk and continue to cook until mixture thickens (about 2 minutes).

Remove from the heat and stir in nutritional yeast, baking powder, vinegar, onion, garlic, pink salt, and pepper.

Fold in shredded Firm "Cheese," chopped kale, and "Sausage" patties.

Transfer mixture into the prepared pan and bake in preheated oven for 25-30 minutes.

Cool in pan for 15 minutes.

---

GLUTEN-FREE | ¾ CUP GLUTEN-FREE FLOUR MIX

# VEGETABLE QUICHE
YIELD: 1 9-INCH QUICHE

⅓ **Piecrust recipe** (or uncooked, vegan pie crust)
**3 tablespoons shortening**
¼ **cup flour** (¼ cup whole wheat)
**1 tablespoon arrowroot powder**
**1 cup almond or rice milk**
½ **cup nutritional yeast**
**3 teaspoons baking powder**
**3 teaspoons vinegar**
**1 teaspoon pink salt**
½ **teaspoon black pepper**
¼ **cup minced red onion**
**2 cups chopped kale**
**1 Eggplant "Burger" patty, chopped**

Preheat oven to 375 degrees.

On a floured board, roll piecrust dough until 13 inches in diameter.
Gently fold the dough in half; lift from underneath and place into pie dish.
Unfold and adjust until dough is centered. Fold excess to fit into the dish,
and using your forefinger, middle finger, and thumb, pinch along the perimeter
to form crimped crust.

In a medium saucepan over medium-high heat, melt shortening. Mix in flour and
arrowroot and cook until small bubbles form. Whisk in almond milk and continue
to cook until mixture thickens (about 2 minutes).

Remove from the heat and stir in nutritional yeast, baking powder, vinegar, pink
salt, and pepper.

Fold in chopped onion, kale, and chopped Eggplant "Burger."

Pour mixture into pie shell and bake in preheated oven until crust is golden brown
(20-25 minutes).

GLUTEN-FREE | 5 tbsp GLUTEN-FREE FLOUR MIX

# "SAUSAGE" BENEDICT
YIELD: 4 SERVINGS

**4 English Muffins** (page 62)
**8 "Sausage" patties**
**6 cups chopped kale**
**1 tablespoon shortening**
**2 cups Hollandaise Sauce** (page 75)

Using a steamer basket, steam kale until just wilted (about 1 minute).

Cut English Muffins in half, spread each side with ¼ teaspoon shortening, and toast under broiler until golden brown.

Place two halves on each of four plates.

Place a warmed "Sausage" patty on each muffin half.

Place equal amounts of kale on each patty.

Cover each half with ¼ cup warm Hollandaise.

Serve immediately.

# "SAUSAGE" BISCUITS
YIELD: 4 "SAUSAGE" BISCUITS

**4 "Chedder" Herb Biscuits** (page 61)
**4 "Sausage" patties**

Preheat oven to 375 degrees.

Gently cut each biscuit in half. Place one "Sausage" patty on one half of each biscuit and return top.

Wrap "Sausage" Biscuits in foil and heat in preheated oven for 15 minutes.

# "MEATBALL" SUBS

YIELD: 4 SANDWICHES

**4 Hamburger Buns (Sub Rolls)**
**16 "Meatballs"**
**1 cup Fresh Herb Marinara**
**1 cup Soft "Cheese"**

Preheat oven to 375 degrees.

Cut each Sub Roll down the side but stopping before the knife goes all the way through. Force each roll open creating a pouch.

Fill each roll with 4 "Meatballs." Cover with ¼ cup Fresh Herb Marinara and then with ¼ cup Soft "Cheese."

Wrap each sandwich in foil.

Heat in preheated oven for 15 minutes.

# VEGETABLE CALZONES

YIELD: 4 CALZONES

1 recipe Pizza Dough
1 cup Fresh Herb Marinara
1 cup Soft "Cheese"
1 cup sliced mushrooms
1 cup chopped Eggplant "Burger," or "Sausage"
2 cups chopped kale

Preheat oven to 415 degrees.

Divide the dough into 4 equal portions.

On a floured board, flatten each dough portion into a circle using your fingers. With your knuckles, gently stretch the dough around its edges, creating a circle until it is approximately 6 inches in diameter. Place on a parchment-lined baking sheet.

Cover each with ¼ cup Fresh Herb Marinara. Spoon ¼ cup of Soft "Cheese" over the sauce. Then layer mushrooms, chopped Eggplant "Burger," and kale over one half of each dough circle.

Fold dough in half, covering filling. Press dough around the edges with your fingers and make indentions around the crust with a fork.

Repeat steps on remaining three calzones.

Bake in preheated oven until tops are browned (15-20 minutes).

---

GLUTEN-FREE | REDUCE FILLING INGREDIENTS BY ¼ CUP, AS GLUTEN-FREE CALZONES WILL BE SMALLER

# GRILLED VEGETABLE AND "CHEESE"

YIELD: 4 SANDWICHES

**1 clove garlic, minced**
**1 cup chopped mushrooms**
**2 cups chopped kale**
**8 pieces of sprouted bread**
**1 cup Soft "Cheese"**
**2 tablespoons grape seed oil**
**1 tablespoon shortening**

In a skillet over medium-high heat, sauté garlic and mushrooms in grape seed oil until cooked through (about 5 minutes).

Remove from heat and toss in chopped kale.

Spread each piece of bread with ⅛ cup Soft "Cheese." Then cover 4 of the bread slices with equal portions of the mushroom/kale mixture.

Make sandwiches by covering with remaining slices.

In the same skillet, melt shortening over medium-high heat.

Place sandwiches in skillet and cook evenly on each side (about 2 minutes).

Serve hot.

# VEGETABLE WRAPS
YIELD: 4 WRAPS

**4 Tortillas**
**½ cup Soft "Cheese"**
**1 cup chopped Eggplant "Burger"**
**1 small avocado, sliced**
**1 small ripe tomato, chopped**
**4 cups mixed greens**
**1 cup Raw-Vegan Ranch** (page 76)

Toss mixed greens in Raw-Vegan Ranch.

Spread ⅛ cup Soft "Cheese" down the middle of each tortilla. Then layer with ¼ cup chopped Eggplant "Burger," followed by avocado slices, tomato, and then mixed greens.

Roll to secure wrap.

# BURRITOS
YIELD: 4 BURRITOS

½ cup cooked black beans
½ teaspoon pink salt
½ teaspoon cumin
1 teaspoon chopped fresh oregano (½ tsp dried oregano)
4 Tortillas
1 cup Soft "Cheese"
1 cup Guacamole (page 97)
1 cup chopped Eggplant "Burger"
2 cups chopped kale
1 cup Enchilada Sauce (page 71)

In a small bowl, mix black beans with pink salt, cumin, and oregano.

Spread ¼ cup Soft "Cheese" down the middle of each tortilla. Then layer each with ⅛ cup seasoned black beans, followed by ¼ cup of Guacamole. Sprinkle each with ¼ cup chopped Eggplant "Burger" and chopped kale. Cover kale with ¼ cup of Enchilada Sauce.

Roll into burritos.

# FALAFEL PITAS
YIELD: 4 SANDWICHES

2 Pitas (page 53)
2 cups Hummus (page 94)
8 Falafels (page 141)
½ cup Raw-Vegan Tzatziki (page 96)

Cut pitas in half. Separate the layers of each pita half to create a pocket.

Spread ½ cup Hummus in each pita pocket.

Stuff two Falafel into each and cover with ⅛ cup Raw-Vegan Tzatziki.

# PHILLY "CHEESE STEAKS"
YIELD: 4 SANDWICHES

**4 Hamburger Buns** (Sub Rolls)
**⅛ cup grape seed oil**
**½ medium red onion, thinly sliced**
**½ medium green pepper, thinly sliced**
**1 cup chopped Eggplant "Burger"**
**1 cup Soft "Cheese"**

Preheat oven to 375 degrees.

Making two angled cuts down the length of each side of the Sub Rolls, create a valley to hold the sandwich fillings.

In a large skillet over medium-high heat, sauté onions and peppers in grape seed oil until tender (about 8 minutes). Add chopped Eggplant "Burger" and cook an additional 2 minutes. Place ¼ of the pepper mixture in the valley of each roll.

Cover each with ¼ cup of Soft "Cheese."

Replace tops, making sandwiches, and wrap in foil.

Heat in preheated oven for 15 minutes.

# "TENDERLOIN" SANDWICHES
YIELD: 4 SANDWICHES

**¾ cup Balsamic Vinaigrette** (page 78)
**2 cups mixed greens**
**8 pieces sprouted bread**
**1 "Tenderloin," sliced** (page 145)
**¼ cup Cashew Cream**
**sliced red onion and sliced tomatoes**

Toss mixed greens in Balsamic Vinaigrette.

Cover each slice of bread with 1 teaspoon of Cashew Cream.

On 4 pieces, layer "Tenderloin" slices, red onion, tomatoes, and mixed greens. Cover with remaining 4 pieces of bread to form sandwiches.

# "CHEESEBURGERS"
YIELD: 4 "CHEESEBURGERS"

**4 Hamburger Buns**
**4 Eggplant "Burger" patties**
**½ cup Soft "Cheese"**
**4 tablespoons ketchup**
**lettuce, tomato, and red onion slices**

Preheat oven to 375 degrees.

Slice hamburger buns in half.

Spread each bun top with ⅛ cup Soft "Cheese." Place patties on bottom halves and cover with prepared tops.

Wrap "Cheeseburgers" in foil and heat in preheated oven for 15 minutes.

Serve with ketchup, lettuce, tomato, and red onion slices.

"Tenderloin" (page 145)

# ENTREES

# ENCHILADAS
YIELD: 6 ENCHILADAS

6 Tortillas
½ medium red onion, cut in thin strips
½ medium green pepper, cut in thin strips
1 cup chopped mushrooms
2 cloves garlic, minced
juice from 1 lime
¼ cup grape seed oil
2 teaspoons cumin
2 tablespoons chopped fresh oregano (1 tbsp dried oregano)
1 teaspoon pink salt
1½ cups cooked brown rice
1½ cups chopped kale
¾ cup Soft "Cheese"
2 cups Enchilada Sauce (page 71)

Preheat oven to 350 degrees.

Grease the bottom of a 9x13-inch baking dish. Then cover with a thin layer of Enchilada Sauce.

In a large bowl, mix onion, green peppers, mushrooms, garlic, lime juice, grape seed oil, cumin, oregano, and pink salt. Marinate mixture for at least 20 minutes.

In a medium-sized bowl, mix brown rice with ½ cup of Enchilada Sauce.

Spread ⅛ cup of Soft "Cheese" down the middle of each tortilla. Then layer ¼ cup seasoned brown rice, ⅓ cup green pepper mixture, and ¼ cup chopped kale. Roll to secure enchilada and place fold-side down into the prepared baking dish.

Repeat until all six are side-by-side in the dish.

Cover with remaining Enchilada Sauce.

Bake in preheated oven for 20 minutes.

Serve with Side Salads (page 173) with Balsamic Vinaigrette (page 78).

# VEGETABLE QUESADILLAS
YIELD: 4 QUESADILLAS

**8 Tortillas**
**1 cup chopped red onion**
**1 cup chopped green pepper**
**1 cup chopped mushrooms**
**1 clove garlic, minced**
**1 tablespoon minced jalapeno** (optional)
**juice from 1 lime**
**¼ cup grape seed oil**
**1 teaspoon cumin**
**1 tablespoon chopped fresh oregano** (1 tsp dried oregano)
**¼ teapoon pink salt**
**2 cups chopped kale**
**1 cup Soft "Cheese"**

In a large bowl, combine onion, green pepper, mushrooms, garlic, jalapeno, lime juice, grape seed oil, cumin, oregano, and pink salt.

Marinate mixture for at least 20 minutes.

In a medium-sized skillet over medium-high heat, saute marinated vegetables until tender (about 5 minutes). Remove from heat and toss in kale.

Cover each tortilla with ⅛ cup Soft "Cheese." Spread ¼ of pepper mixture on 4 of the tortillas. Cover with remaining tortillas.

Preheat skillet or griddle over medium heat (about 5 minutes).

Place each quesadilla onto the hot skillet and cook until browned on each side (about 2 minutes per side).

Serve with Guacamole (page 97) and Pico de Gallo (page 97).

# SOFT TACOS
YIELD: 4 TACOS

4 Tortillas
⅛ cup grape seed oil
¼ cup minced red onion
½ teaspoon minced garlic
2 cups chopped Eggplant "Burger"
1 teaspoon cumin
1 tablespoon chopped fresh oregano (1 tsp dried oregano)
2 cups chopped kale
1½ cups grated Firm "Cheese"
1 cup Guacamole (page 97)
1 cup Pico de Gallo (page 97)

In a skillet over medium-high heat, sauté onion and garlic in grape seed oil until tender (about 5 minutes). Add chopped Eggplant "Burger," cumin, and oregano and continue to cook for 2 minutes.

Remove from heat and toss in kale.

Sprinkle 3 tablespoons of grated Firm "Cheese" down the middle of each tortilla. Cover with ½ cup of Eggplant "Burger" mixture. Then layer with ¼ cup Guacamole and ¼ cup of Pico de Gallo.

Fold tortillas to make tacos.

Serve with Refried Black Beans (page 172).

# BLACK BEAN BURGERS
YIELD: 4 BURGERS

**2 cups cooked black beans**
**1 cup cooked brown rice**
**⅓ cup chopped red onion**
**1 teaspoon minced garlic**
**⅓ cup chopped carrots**
**¼ cup arrowroot**
**2 tablespoons flour** (2 tbsp whole wheat)
**1 teaspoon chili powder**
**1 teaspoon cumin**
**1 tablespoon chopped fresh oregano** (1 tsp dried oregano)
**2 cups chopped kale**

Preheat oven to 375 degrees.

In a large mixing bowl, mash black beans and brown rice with a potato masher until combined.

Mix in onions, garlic, carrots, arrowroot, flour, chili powder, cumin, and oregano. Fold in kale.

Form four patties with your hands and place onto a parchment-lined baking sheet.

Bake in preheated oven for 20 minutes (10 minutes on each side).

Serve over Spanish Brown Rice (page 171).

GLUTEN-FREE | 3 tbsp GLUTEN-FREE FLOUR MIX

# WHITE BEAN PIMENTO "CHEESE" BURGERS

YIELD: 4 BURGERS

1 medium red pepper (or ½ cup pimentos)
grape seed oil
2 cups cooked white beans
1 cup cooked brown rice
1 clove garlic, minced
6 tablespoons nutritional yeast
3 tablespoons arrowroot
½ teaspoon pink salt
2 cups chopped kale

ROAST PEPPER
Preheat oven to 450 degrees.

Cover red pepper with grape seed oil. Place onto a baking sheet lined with foil. Roast for 30 minutes, turning pepper with tongs after 15 minutes.

Remove and immediately wrap roasted pepper in foil. Let sit 30 minutes.

Cut cooled peppers into quarters, remove skins, and dice. Save juices from the bottom of the foil.

Preheat oven to 375 degrees.

Place white beans, brown rice, garlic, nutritional yeast, arrowroot, and pink salt into a food processor (with S blade) or blender and blend until smooth.

Fold in kale and diced roasted red pepper.

Form 4 patties with your hands and place onto a parchment-lined baking sheet.

Bake in preheated oven for 20 minutes (10 minutes on each side).

Serve over Cajun Brown Rice (page 169).

# WAKAME CAKES
YIELD: 8 CAKES

¼ cup wakame
¼ cup grape seed oil
1 cup minced red onion
1 teaspoon minced garlic
1½ cups diced celery
¾ cup chopped red pepper
1½ cups chopped mushrooms
1 cup cooked brown rice
1 tablespoon apple cider vinegar
6 tablespoons arrowroot powder
½ teaspoon paprika
1 teaspoon minced ginger
¼ teaspoon allspice
⅛ teaspoon nutmeg
pinch ground cloves
1 teaspoon pink salt
1 teaspoon dijon mustard
1 teaspoon black pepper
¼ cup chopped parsley

Rinse wakame. In a small bowl, cover with water and soak for 15 minutes. Rinse again.

In a large skillet over medium-high heat, sauté onions, garlic, celery, peppers, and mushrooms in ⅛ cup of grape seed oil until tender (about 8 minutes).

Place brown rice, vinegar, arrowroot, paprika, ginger, allspice, nutmeg, cloves, pink salt, and mustard into a food processor (with S blade) or blender and blend until smooth.

Fold in onion mixture, parsley, wakame, and black pepper. Form into 8 patties.

Heat remaining grape seed oil in a large skillet over medium heat. Place Wakame Cakes into hot oil and cook 3 minutes on each side.

Place on a baking sheet lined with paper towels or paper bags to absorb excess oil.

Serve over mixed greens with Balsamic Vinaigrette (page 78).

# FALAFEL
YIELD: 24 FALAFEL

**2 cups cooked chickpeas**
**1 clove garlic, minced**
**2 tablespoons flour** (2 tbsp whole wheat)
**1 tablespoon grape seed oil**
**1 teaspoon apple cider vinegar**
**1 teaspoon baking powder**
**1 teaspoon cumin**
**1 teapoon pink salt**
**1 small onion, chopped**
**1 tablespoon minced parsley**

Preheat oven to 350 degrees.

Place chickpeas, garlic, flour, grape seed oil, vinegar, baking powder, cumin, and pink salt into a food processor (with S blade) or blender and blend until smooth.

Add onion and parsley and pulse several times to incorporate.

Spoon ⅛ cup-sized balls of mixture onto a parchment-lined baking sheet.

Bake in preheated oven for 15-20 minutes.

Serve with Pita (page 53), Baba Ganoush (page 96), and Side Salads (page 173) with Raw Vegan Tzatziki (page 96).

GLUTEN-FREE | 3 tbsp GLUTEN-FREE FLOUR MIX

# JAMAICAN JERK BLACK EYED PEA FRITTERS
YIELD: 24 FRITTERS

**2 cups cooked black eyed peas**
**1 cup cooked brown rice**
**1 clove garlic, minced**
**2 tablespoons arrowroot powder**
**1 teaspoon jerk seasoning**
**1 teaspoon pink salt**
**2 cups Jerk Sauce (page 72)**

Preheat oven to 375 degrees.

Place black eyed peas, brown rice, garlic, arrowroot, jerk seasoning, and pink salt into a food processor (with S blade) or blender and puree.

Make ⅛ cup-sized patty shapes and place onto a parchment-lined baking sheet.

Bake in preheated oven for 20 minutes.

Cover with Jerk Sauce.

Serve with Caribbean Sweet Potatoes and Pineapple (page 164) and Southern Steamed Collard Greens (page 176).

# "MEATLOAF"
YIELD: 2 LOAVES

2 cups Eggplant Puree
2 cloves garlic, minced
1 tablespoon chopped fresh thyme (1 tsp dried thyme)
1 teaspoon marjoram
1 teaspoon pink salt
1 teaspoon black pepper
1 tablespoon dijon mustard
⅓ cup ketchup
2 cups brown rice
¼ cup arrowroot powder
2 tablespoons flour (2 tbsp whole wheat)
1 small red onion, minced
½ cup mushrooms, diced
1 cup carrots, diced
½ cup chopped green pepper
2 cups chopped kale
½ cup ketchup for sauce

Preheat oven to 375 degrees.

Place Eggplant Puree, garlic, thyme, marjoram, pink salt, pepper, mustard and ketchup into a food processor (with S blade) or blender, and blend until smooth. Add brown rice, arrowroot, and flour, and continue to blend.

Transfer mixture to a large bowl and fold in onion, mushrooms, carrots, green pepper, and kale.

Form two loaf shapes on a parchment-lined baking sheet.

Bake in preheated oven for 25-30 minutes.

Remove and cover tops with ¼ cup ketchup each.

Return to the oven and bake an additional 5 minutes.

Serve with Scalloped Sweet Potatoes (page 168) and Side Salads (page 182).

GLUTEN-FREE | 3 tbsp GLUTEN-FREE FLOUR MIX

# "TENDERLOIN"
YIELD: 2 "TENDERLOINS"

1 cup mushrooms, minced
3 cloves garlic, minced
1 tablespoon grape seed oil
2 cups Pureed Eggplant
2 cups cooked brown rice
⅛ cup shortening
½ cup onion, minced
2 tablespoons coconut aminos (or tamari)
2 tablespoons chopped fresh thyme (1 tbsp dried thyme)
2 teaspoons marjoram
6 tablespoons arrowroot powder
2 tablespoons flour (2 tablespoons whole wheat)
1 teaspoon black pepper

Preheat oven to 375 degrees.

In a small skillet over medium-high heat, saute mushrooms and 1 clove minced garlic in grape seed oil until tender (about 5 minutes).

In a food processor (with S blade) or blender, blend Pureed Eggplant, brown rice, sauteed mushrooms, remaining garlic, shortening, onion, coconut aminos, thyme, and marjoram, until smooth.

Blend in arrowroot until incorporated.

Stir in black pepper.

Form two tenderloin shapes on a parchment-lined baking sheet.

Bake in preheated oven for 25-30 minutes.

Serve with Mashed Sweet Potatoes (page 164) and Steamed Southern Collard Greens (page 176).

GLUTEN-FREE | 3 tbsp GLUTEN-FREE FLOUR MIX

For more firm "Tenderloin," refrigerate for one hour before serving , then reheat.

# LOADED SWEET POTATO

YIELD: 4 SERVINGS

**2 large sweet potatoes**
**1 tablespoon grape seed oil**
**¾ teaspoon pink salt**
**2 tablespoons shortening**
**¼ cup chopped fresh chives (2 tbsp dried chives)**
**1 cup chopped broccoli**
**1 cup chopped Eggplant "Burger"**
**1 cup Soft "Cheese"**

Preheat oven to 415 degrees.

Line a 9x13-inch baking dish with foil.

Cover washed sweet potatoes with grape seed oil and dust with ¼ teaspoon of pink salt until entire skins are covered. Place in baking dish and bake uncovered until soft (about one hour).

Remove potatoes from the oven and reduce heat to 350 degrees.

Carefully spoon hot flesh from skins, leaving enough for the skins to their hold shape.

Place potato flesh into a large mixing bowl. Add the shortening and remaining pink salt and mash using potato masher. Fold in chives. Spoon ¼ of potato mixture into each skin.

Steam chopped broccoli until just tender (about 2 minutes).

Cover each potato with ¼ cup steamed broccoli, then ¼ cup chopped Eggplant "Burger." Top potatoes with ¼ cup Soft "Cheese."

Bake in preheated oven for 15 minutes.

Serve with a Side Salad (page 182) or a cup of Lentil Soup (page 86).

# SHEPARD'S PIE
YIELD: SERVES 6

2 medium-sized sweet potatoes
¼ cup grape seed oil
1 teaspoon baking powder
½ teaspoon pink salt
⅛ cup minced red onion
1 teaspoon apple cider vinegar
1 medium onion, chopped
1 clove garlic, minced
3 medium sized carrots, chopped
3 ribs celery, chopped
1 cup chopped zucchini
2 cups chopped mushrooms
1 teaspoon coconut aminos (or tamari)
1 tablespoon ketchup
2 tablespoons flour (2 tablespoons whole wheat)
2 tablespoons arrowroot powder
1 teaspoon black pepper

Preheat oven to 375 degrees.

Grease a 9x13-inch baking dish.

Cut sweet potatoes into ¼-inch slices.

Place potatoes into a large soup pot and cover with water. Cook over medium-high heat until tender (about 25 minutes).

Drain potatoes and place in a large bowl. Add 1 tablespoon grape seed oil and mash with a potato masher until smooth. Add baking powder, pink salt, ⅛ cup minced red onion, and vinegar. Set aside.

In a large skillet over medium-high heat, sauté chopped onion, garlic, carrots, celery, zucchini, and mushrooms in remaining grape seed oil until cooked through (about 10 minutes).

Remove from heat. Mix in coconut aminos, ketchup, flour, arrowroot, and black pepper.

Pour mixture into the prepared baking dish. Spoon the sweet potato mixture over the top.

Bake in preheated oven for 20 minutes.

GLUTEN-FREE | 3 tbsp GLUTEN-FREE FLOUR MIX

# BROWN RICE "BURGER" CASSEROLE
YIELD: 6 SERVINGS

4 cups cooked brown rice
2 cups Soft "Cheese"
½ cup Vegetable Stock
1 teaspoon pink salt
2 cups chopped Eggplant "Burger"
4 cups chopped kale

Preheat oven to 350 degrees.

In a large mixing bowl, combine brown rice, Soft "Cheese," Vegetable Stock, and pink salt.

Fold in Eggplant "Burger" and kale.

Spoon mixture into a 9x13-inch casserole dish.

Bake in preheated oven for 20 minutes.

# THAI MUSHROOM STIR FRY
YIELD: 4 SERVINGS

¼ cup grape seed oil
1 cup chopped mushrooms
1 clove garlic, minced
½ medium red onion, chopped
½ red pepper, chopped
2 cups shredded cabbage
2 cups Thai Peanut Sauce (page 73)
4 cups chopped kale
4 cups cooked brown rice

In a large skillet over medium-high heat, sauté mushrooms, garlic, onion, red pepper, and cabbage in grape seed oil until tender (about 8 minutes).

Reduce heat to low and add Thai Peanut Sauce. Toss in kale.

Serve over cooked brown rice.

# SESAME MUSHROOMS

YIELD: 4 SERVINGS

**2 cups button mushrooms, stems trimmed**
**⅛ cup grape seed oil**
**2 cloves garlic, minced**
**2 tablespoons flour** (2 tbsp whole wheat)
**2 tablespoons arrowroot powder**
**¼ teaspoon baking soda**
**½ teaspoon pink salt**
**2 tablespoons water**
**2 tablespoons coconut aminos** (or tamari)
**2 cups Asian Sesame Sauce** (page 74)

Preheat oven to 375 degrees.

In a large skillet over medium-high heat, sauté garlic and mushrooms in grape seed oil until softened (about 5 minutes).

In a medium-sized bowl, whisk flour, arrowroot, baking soda, pink salt, coconut aminos, and water. Pour mushrooms and excess oil into the bowl. Toss to coat and chill in the refrigerator for 20 minutes. Spread onto a parchment-lined baking sheet and bake in preheated oven for 20 minutes.

Cover with Asian Sesame Sauce.

Serve over brown rice.

---

GLUTEN-FREE | 3 tbsp GLUTEN-FREE FLOUR MIX

---

# VEGETABLE CURRY
YIELD: 4 SERVINGS

⅓ cup grape seed oil
1 small red onion, chopped
2 cloves garlic, minced
½ medium sweet potato, cubed
½ medium eggplant, cubed
½ green pepper, chopped
½ red pepper, chopped
1 medium carrot, chopped
½ zucchini, chopped
1 cup cooked chickpeas
½ cup orange juice
1 cup Vegetable Stock
½ teaspoon turmeric
1 tablespoon curry
½ teaspoon cinnamon
½ teaspoon cayenne pepper
½ teaspoon pink salt
2 cups chopped kale
4 cups cooked brown rice

In a large saucepan over medium-high heat, sauté onion, garlic, sweet potatoes, eggplant, green and red peppers, carrots, and zucchini in grape seed oil until tender (about 10 minutes).

Add chickpeas, orange juice, Vegetable Stock, turmeric, curry, cinnamon, cayenne, and pink salt.

Reduce heat to low, cover, and simmer for 20 minutes.

Fold in kale.

Serve over brown rice.

# VEGETABLE TERIYAKI
YIELD: 4 SERVINGS

¼ cup grape seed oil
1 medium onion, chopped
1 clove garlic, minced
1½ cups chopped mushrooms
1 medium zucchini, chopped
1 medium carrot, chopped
1 medium daikon, chopped
1 medium bok choy, chopped
1 cup bean sprouts
1½ cups Teriyaki Sauce (page 73)
4 cups cooked brown rice

In a large skillet over medium-high heat, sauté onion, garlic, and mushrooms in grape seed oil until softened (about 5 minutes). Add zucchini, carrot, daikon, and bok choy. Continue to cook for 5 minutes.

Add bean sprouts and Teriyaki Sauce.

Reduce heat to low, cover, and simmer for 10 minutes.

Serve over brown rice.

# MOUSAKKA
YIELD: SERVES 6

2 medium eggplants
2 medium sweet potatoes
½ cup grape seed oil
¾ cup flour (¾ cup whole wheat)
¼ teaspoon pink salt
1 medium red onion, chopped
2 cloves garlic, minced
½ cup Vegetable Stock
1 teaspoon cinnamon
¼ teaspoon allspice
1 teaspoon sugar
1 cup diced tomatoes
2 tablespoons tomato paste
¼ cup chopped parsley
2 cups chopped Eggplant "Burger"
2 cups chopped kale
2 cups Béchamel Sauce (page 75)
1 teaspoon baking powder
1 teaspoon apple cider vinegar

GLUTEN-FREE | 1 CUP GLUTEN-FREE FLOUR MIX

Preheat oven to 400 degrees.

### PREPARE EGGPLANT
Remove very tops of eggplants and slice lengthwise into ½-inch slices. Rub the slices with ¼ cup grape seed oil and place into a foil-lined baking dish. Roast for 20 minutes.

Mix ¾ cup flour with ¼ teaspoon pink salt. Take roasted eggplant slices and dredge each in salted flour. Place onto wax paper until ready to use.

### PREPARE SWEET POTATOES
Cut sweet potatoes into ¼-inch slices. Place into a large saucepan and cover with water. Bring to a boil over medium-high heat and cook until just tender (about 20 minutes).

### MAKE "MEAT" SAUCE
In a large skillet over medium-high heat, sauté onion and garlic in remaining ¼ cup of grape seed oil until transparent (about 5 minutes). Add broth, cinnamon, allspice, sugar, diced tomatoes, tomato paste, and parsley.

Reduce heat to low and simmer for 20 minutes. Remove from heat and toss in Eggplant "Burger" and kale.

### ASSEMBLE
Reduce oven temperature to 350 degrees.

Grease and flour a 9x13-inch baking dish.

Cover the bottom of the baking dish with sweet potato slices. Top with a layer of eggplant slices. Add "meat" sauce and then another layer of eggplant.

Mix the Béchamel Sauce with 1 teaspoon baking powder and 1 teaspoon vinegar and spread over the eggplant layer.

Bake in preheated oven for 20 minutes.

Serve with Side Salads (page 173) and Raw-Vegan Tzatziki (page 96).

# VEGETABLE LASAGNE
YIELD: SERVES 6

1 package brown rice lasagne noodles
3 cups Fresh Herb Marinara
2 cups Soft "Cheese"
2 cups sliced mushrooms
2 cups chopped Eggplant "Burger"
4 cups chopped kale
¼ cup grated Firm "Cheese" (optional)

Preheat oven to 375 degrees.

Cook brown rice lasagne noodles according to package directions. Drain.

Lightly coat the bottom of a 9x13-inch baking dish with Fresh Herb Marinara.

Begin a layering pattern with the bottom layer brown rice noodles. Cover with Fresh Herb Marinara, Soft "Cheese," mushrooms, chopped Eggplant "Burger," kale, and more Fresh Herb Marinara. Continue layering until all ingredients are used.

Cover top with Fresh Herb Marinara and sprinkle with grated Firm "Cheese."

Bake in preheated oven for 20-25 minutes.

Serve with Side Salads (page 173) and Italian Dressing (page 78).

# MUSHROOM RAVIOLI
YIELD: SERVES 4

**PASTA**
**2 cups flour** (1¾ cups whole wheat)
**1 teaspoon pink salt**
**2 tablespoons chopped fresh basil** (1 tbsp dried basil)
**2 tablespoons chopped fresh oregano** (1 tbsp dried oregano)
**1 teaspoon grape seed oil**
**½ cup water**

**FILLING**
**1 tablespoon grape seed oil**
**½ clove garlic, minced**
**¼ cup minced mushrooms**
**¼ cup Soft "Cheese"**
**¼ cup minced kale**

**2 cups Fresh Herb Marinara**

---

GLUTEN-FREE | 2½ CUPS GLUTEN-FREE FLOUR MIX | 2 tsp XANTHAN GUM

## MAKE PASTA
In a large mixing bowl, combine flour, salt, basil, and oregano. Stir in grape seed oil and water. Using the dough hook on a standing mixer, or your hands on a floured board, knead dough for 5 minutes. Dough should be smooth and elastic.

## MAKE FILLING
In a medium skillet over medium-high heat, sauté garlic and mushrooms in grape seed oil until cooked through (about 2 minutes).

Transfer mixture to a medium-sized bowl and combine with Soft "Cheese."

Divide dough into two equal sections.

On a lightly floured board, roll each piece of dough into a paper-thin rectangular shape, doing your best to make them the same shape.

Spoon ¼ teaspoon dollups of filling onto one layer, leaving 1½-inch squares around each.

Using your finger or a pastry brush, trace a grid around fillings with water. This will help the top layer stick. Gently pick up the other layer of pasta and carefully place on top of fillings. Using the sides of your hands, press layers against one another around the fillings where you traced the water.

Using a pastry cutter or a sharp knife, cut ravioli on the same traced line. Place on wax or parchment paper until ready to cook.

In a large soup pot over medium-high heat, bring 3 quarts of water to a boil. Add ravioli one layer at a time and cook until done (about 5 minutes). Remove with a slotted spoon and drain.

Cover with Fresh Herb Marinara.

# "SAUSAGE" KALE PIZZA
YIELD: 1 12-INCH PIZZA

½ recipe Pizza Dough (or 1 12-inch vegan pizza crust)
1 cup Fresh Herb Marinara
1 cup grated Firm "Cheese"
½ cup sliced mushrooms
1 cup chopped "Sausage"
2 cups chopped kale

Preheat oven to 415 degrees.

Roll dough on a lightly floured board, forming a circle, until ¼-inch thick. Using your knuckles, gently stretch dough around its edges, creating crust, until approximately 12 inches. Place dough onto a parchment-lined baking sheet. Once on the baking sheet, the dough can be reshaped. Do not overwork!

Cover crust with Fresh Herb Marinara. Sprinkle with grated Firm "Cheese." Evenly cover with mushrooms, chopped "Sausage," and kale.

Bake in preheated oven for 15-20 minutes until crust is golden brown.

# SPAGHETTI AND "MEATBALLS"
YIELD: SERVES 4

20 "Meatballs"
2 cups cooked brown rice noodles
2 cups Vodka Sauce (page 70) or Fresh Herb Marinara
½ cup grated Firm "Cheese"

Place five "Meatballs" on top of ½ cup brown rice noodles. Cover with ½ cup of Vodka sauce.

Sprinkle with grated Firm "Cheese."

Serve with Side Salads (page 173) and Italian Dressing (page 78).

# WILD MUSHROOM CREPES
YIELD: SERVES 4

**4 Crepes** (page 59)
**FILLING**
**⅛ cup grape seed oil**
**1 clove garlic, minced**
**¼ cup minced red onion**
**1 cup chopped wild mushrooms**
**1 cup chopped white mushrooms**
**4 cups chopped kale**
**SAUCE**
**3 tablespoons shortening**
**⅛ cup flour** (⅛ cup whole wheat)
**1 cup almond or rice milk**
**2 cloves garlic, minced**
**¼ cup white wine**
**½ cup Vegetable Stock**
**1 teaspoon pink salt**
**1 teaspoon black pepper**

MAKE FILLING
In a large skillet over medium-high heat, sauté garlic, onion, and mushrooms in grape seed oil until cooked through (about 5 minutes).
Remove from heat and toss in kale.

MAKE SAUCE
In a medium saucepan over medium-high heat, melt shortening. Mix in flour with a spatula until incorporated and continue to cook until small bubbles form. Whisk in almond milk until smooth. Continue to stir until mixture thickens (about 2 minutes).

In a medium skillet over medium-high heat, melt shortening and sauté garlic for 1 minute. Reduce heat to medium-low, add wine and Vegetable Stock, and simmer for 20 minutes.

Add almond milk mixture and whisk.

Cover until ready to use.

TO ASSEMBLE
Spread ¼ of the filling onto the bottom half of each crepe and fold over. Cover with ½ cup sauce.

GLUTEN-FREE | 3 tbsp GLUTEN-FREE FLOUR MIX

# SIDES
# and
# SALADS

# MASHED SWEET POTATOES
YIELD: SERVES 4

2 medium sweet potatoes
⅛ cup shortening
⅛ cup almond or rice milk
½ teaspoon pink salt
1 teaspoon pepper
¼ cup chopped chives (optional)

Cut sweet potatoes into ¼-inch pieces. Place into a large saucepan and cover with water. Cook over medium-high heat until soft (about 25 minutes).

Drain and place into a large bowl. Add shortening and mash with potato masher until smooth.

Add almond milk, pink salt, pepper, and chives.

Whisk until fully incorporated and silky in texture.


# CARIBBEAN SWEET POTATOES WITH PINEAPPLE
YIELD: SERVES 4

¼ cup shortening
⅛ cup brown sugar
1 teaspoon minced ginger
¼ cup chopped cilantro
½ teaspoon pink salt
2 medium sweet potatoes
1 cup chopped pineapple

Preheat oven to 400 degrees.

In a small bowl, combine shortening, brown sugar, ginger, cilantro, and pink salt.

Cut sweet potatoes into ½-inch slices. Then cut the slices into fourths and place into a large mixing bowl. Add chopped pineapple.

Using your hands, cover the potatoes and pineapple with the shortening mixture.

Place into a foil-lined baking dish.

Bake in preheated oven until potatoes are tender (35-40 minutes).

# HERB ROASTED SWEET POTATOES
YIELD: SERVES 4

**2 medium sweet potatoes**
**⅛ cup grape seed oil**
**2 tablespoons dijon mustard**
**2 teaspoons fresh thyme, chopped**
**1 clove garlic, minced**
**1 teaspoon fresh rosemary, chopped**
**1 teaspoon pink salt**
**½ teaspoon black pepper**

Preheat oven to 400 degrees.

Line a 9x13-inch baking dish with foil.

Cut sweet potatoes into ½-inch slices. Then cut the slices into fourths and place into a large mixing bowl.

In a small bowl, whisk together grape seed oil, mustard, thyme, garlic, rosemary, pink salt, and pepper.

Pour mixture over sweet potatoes and toss until all are covered.

Transfer to the prepared baking dish and roast in preheated oven until soft (about 35-40 minutes).

# CAJUN SWEET POTATO FRIES
YIELD: SERVES 4

1 large sweet potato
⅛ cup grape seed oil
1 teaspoon minced garlic
2 tablespoons paprika
⅛ teaspoon cayenne pepper
¼ teaspoon pink salt
¼ teaspoon pepper

Preheat oven to 400 degrees.

Cut sweet potato into fry shapes.

In a large bowl, toss fries in grape seed oil and garlic until all are coated.

In a small bowl, combine paprika, cayenne, pink salt, and pepper. Sprinkle over the fries and toss.

Place onto a foil-lined baking sheet and bake in preheated oven for 15 minutes.

Turn off the oven and leave fries in decreasing heat for 30 minutes.

# SCALLOPED SWEET POTATOES

YIELD: SERVES 6

2 medium sweet potatoes
2 cups Béchamel Sauce (page 75)
2 cups grated Firm "Cheese"
½ cup Vegetable Stock
pink salt and pepper

Preheat oven to 375 degrees.

Grease a 2-quart baking dish.

Cut sweet potatoes into very thin slices (about ⅛-inch). Begin a layering pattern by placing a layer of sweet potato slices at the bottom of the prepared baking dish. Cover the potatoes with Béchamel Sauce. Then sprinkle with grated Firm "Cheese." Continue pattern until all ingredients have been used.

Pour Vegetable Stock over completed casserole.

Bake in preheated oven for 25-30 minutes.

# BROWN RICE MACARONI AND "CHEESE"

YIELD: SERVES 4

4 cups cooked brown rice macaroni
½ cup Soft "Cheese"
1 cup almond or rice milk
2 tablespoons nutritional yeast
1 tablespoon minced red onion
½ teaspoon minced garlic
1 teaspoon paprika
½ teaspoon pink salt

In a large saucepan over medium-low heat, combine brown rice macaroni, Soft "Cheese," almond milk, nutritional yeast, onion, garlic, paprika, and pink salt.

Mix until creamy.

# CAJUN BROWN RICE
YIELD: SERVES 4

2 cups cooked brown rice
½ cup Vegetable Stock
¼ cup minced red onion
1 teaspoon minced garlic
1 tablespoon paprika
1 tablespoon chopped fresh oregano (1 tsp dried oregano)
1 teaspoon chopped fresh thyme (½ tsp dried thyme)
¼- ½ teaspoon crushed red pepper
½ teaspoon pink salt
1 teaspoon pepper
¾ cup chopped "Sausage"

In a large saucepan over medium-low heat, combine brown rice, Vegetable Stock, onion, garlic, paprika, oregano, thyme, red pepper, pink salt, and pepper.

Fold in chopped "Sausage."

Reduce heat to low, cover, and simmer for 10 minutes.

# FRIED BROWN RICE
YIELD: SERVES 4

1 tablespoon Tahini
3 tablespoons coconut aminos (or tamari)
⅛ cup Vegetable Stock
3 tablespoons grape seed oil
¾ cup chopped red onion
½ teaspoon minced garlic
½ cup chopped carrots
2 cups bean sprouts
2 cups cooked brown rice
4 green onions, chopped
2 cups chopped kale

In a small bowl, whisk together Tahini, coconut aminos, and Vegetable Stock.

In a large saucepan over medium-high heat, sauté onions, garlic, carrots, and sprouts in grape seed oil until tender (about 3 minutes).

Reduce heat to low and add brown rice and Tahini sauce.

Fold in kale and green onions and cover for 10 minutes.

# SPANISH BROWN RICE
YIELD: SERVES 4

⅛ cup grape seed oil
½ cup chopped red onion
½ teaspoon minced garlic
½ jalapeno, diced
2 cups cooked brown rice
1 cup tomato sauce
¼ cup water
1 teaspoon cumin
1 tablespoon chopped fresh oregano (1 tsp dried oregano)
1 teaspoon pink salt
2 cups chopped kale

In a large saucepan over medium-high heat, sauté onion, garlic, and jalapeno in grape seed oil until tender (about 5 minutes).

Reduce heat to low. Add brown rice, tomato sauce, water, cumin, oregano, and pink salt.

Toss in kale.

# QUINOA LENTIL SALAD
YIELD: SERVES 4

1 cup cooked quinoa
1 cup cooked lentils
¼ cup minced red onion
½ cup chopped green peppers
½ cup chopped cucumber
1 cup Balsamic Vinaigrette (page 78)

In a large mixing bowl, combine quinoa, lentils, onion, green peppers, and cucumber.

Add Balsamic Vinaigrette and toss.

# BAKED BLACK BEANS
YIELD: SERVES 6

4 cups cooked black beans
1 small red onion, thinly sliced
3 tablespoons brown sugar
¼ cup ketchup
⅛ cup mustard
¼ teaspoon crushed red pepper
1 teaspoon pink salt
1 teaspoon black pepper
¼ cup Vegetable Stock

Preheat oven to 350 degrees.

In a large mixing bowl, combine black beans, sliced onion, brown sugar, ketchup, mustard, crushed red pepper, pink salt, pepper, and Vegetable Stock.

Pour mixture into a 2-quart baking dish.

Bake in preheated oven until onions are tender (30-35 minutes).

# REFRIED BLACK BEANS
YIELD: SERVES 4

3 tablespoons shortening
½ cup minced red onion
2 cups cooked black beans
¼ cup water
½ teaspoon pink salt

In a large skillet, melt 3 tablespoons shortening and sauté minced red onion until tender (about 3 minutes).

Add beans and mash with a potato masher until smooth.

Stir in water and pink salt.

# SEAWEED SALAD
YIELD: SERVES 4

½ cup dried wakame
3 tablespoons apple cider vinegar
3 tablespoons coconut aminos (or tamari)
2 tablespoons Tahini
1 tablespoon grapeseed oil
1 tablespoon agave
1 tablespoon minced ginger
½ teaspoon minced garlic
2 green onions, sliced
¼ teaspoon red pepper flakes

Rinse wakame. In a small bowl, cover with water and soak for 15 minutes. Rinse again.

In a medium-sized bowl, whisk together vinegar, coconut aminos, Tahini, grape seed oil, ginger, garlic, green onions, and red pepper flakes.

Toss in wakame.

# SIDE SALAD
YIELD: SERVES 4

4 cups mixed greens
2 cups chopped kale
1 cup chopped cucumber
¼ cup chopped green onion
1 avocado, cubed
1 cup dressing

In a large bowl, combine mixed greens, kale, cucumber, green onions, and avocado.

Add dressing of choice and toss.

# VEGETABLE QUINOA
YIELD: SERVES 4

**3 tablespoons grape seed oil**
**½ cup diced red onion**
**1 teaspoon minced garlic**
**1 cup chopped mushrooms**
**2 cups cooked quinoa**
**¼ cup Vegetable Stock**
**2 cups chopped kale**
**1 tablespoon coconut aminos** (or tamari)

In a large saucepan over medium-high heat, sauté onion, garlic, and mushrooms in grape seed oil until tender (about 5 minutes).

Add quinoa, Vegetable Stock, kale, and coconut aminos.

# SOUTHERN STEAMED COLLARD GREENS
YIELD: SERVES 4

1 large bunch of collard greens

**SAUCE**
2 cups light vegan beer
2 tablespoons sugar
½ cup apple cider vinegar
2 tablespoons Vegetable Boullion Paste (page 42)
½ teaspoon crushed red pepper
2 teaspoons pink salt
1 teaspoon pepper

MAKE SAUCE
In a small saucepan over medium heat, combine beer, sugar, vinegar, and bouillon paste.

Bring to a boil. Reduce heat to low and simmer for 20 minutes. Add crushed red pepper, pink salt, and pepper.

Chop collards into 2-inch strips and place into a steamer basket over boiling water.

Cover and steam until just tender (about 2 minutes).

Remove immediately and place into a large bowl.

Toss in sauce.

# BRAISED RED CABBAGE
YIELD: SERVES 4

⅛ cup grape seed oil
½ medium red onion, thinly sliced
1 bay leaf
1 cinnamon stick
½ small head red cabbage, thinly sliced
½ apple, thinly sliced
1 cup Vegetable Stock
⅛ cup apple cider vinegar
1 tablespoon sugar
½ teaspoon pink salt
½ teaspoon pepper

In a large skillet over medium-high heat, sauté onion, bay leaf, and cinnamon stick in grape seed oil until onions are tender (about 5 minutes).

Stir in cabbage and cook until softened (about 5 minutes).

Add sliced apple, Vegetable Stock, vinegar, and sugar.

Reduce heat to low, cover, and simmer for 35 minutes.

Remove cinnamon stick and bay leaf.

Raise heat to medium-high and boil for 5 minutes so the sauce can reduce.

Add pink salt and pepper.

# WHITE BEAN KALE SALAD
YIELD: SERVES 4

½ cup Tahini
¼ cup grape seed oil
1 tablespoon agave
1 clove garlic, minced
juice from 1 lemon
⅛- ¼ cup water
1 teaspoon chopped fresh thyme (½ tsp dried thyme)
½ teaspoon pink salt
2 cups cooked white beans
4 cups chopped kale
½ avocado, cubed

MAKE DRESSING
Place tahini, grape seed oil, agave, garlic, lemon juice, water, thyme, and pink salt into the container of a high-powdered blender.

Blend until smooth.

In a large bowl, combine beans, kale, and avocado.

Add dressing and toss.

# SALAD NICOISE
YIELD: SERVES 4

1 medium sweet potato, cubed
1 clove garlic, minced
2 tablespoons grape seed oil
2 cups cooked white beans
6 cups mixed greens
1 small yellow onion, thinly sliced
2 cups chopped ripe tomato
1½ cups steamed green beans
1 avocado, cubed
1 cup Citrus Vinaigrette (page 79)
fresh ground pepper
pink salt

In a large saucepan over medium-high heat, boil cubed sweet potatoes until tender (about 20 minutes). Remove with slotted spoon and set aside.

In a medium skillet over medium-high heat, sauté garlic in grape seed oil for 1 minute. Add white beans and cook an additional 2 minutes. Set aside.

Divide greens between 4 pasta bowls. Spread sliced onions over greens. Arrange the sweet potatoes, tomatoes, white beans, steamed green beans, and avocado in mounds over the mixed greens.

Drizzle ¼ cup Citrus Vinaigrette over each salad.

Dress with fresh ground black pepper and pink salt.

# MIXED VEGETABLE SALAD
YIELD: SERVES 4

8 cups mixed greens
4 cups chopped kale
1 cup chopped carrots
1 cup chopped cucumber
1 cup chopped celery
½ green pepper, chopped
1 avocado, cubed
1 cup Raw-Vegan Ranch (page 76)

In a large bowl, combine mixed greens, kale, carrots, cucumber, celery, green peppers, and avocado.

Add Raw-Vegan Ranch and toss.


# RAW GUACAMOLE KALE SALAD
YIELD: SERVES 4

6 cups chopped kale
2 cups Guacamole (page 97)

Place kale and Guacamole into a large bowl and toss.


# RAW-VEGAN COLESLAW
YIELD: SERVES 4

4 cups shredded cabbage
2 cups chopped kale
1½ cups Cashew Cream
1½ teaspoons pink salt
1½ teaspoons pepper

In a large mixing bowl, combine cabbage, kale, Cashew Cream, pink salt, and pepper.

# DESSERTS

# "CUSTARD"
YIELD: 1 ½ CUPS

**3 tablespoons shortening**
**¼ cup flour** (¼ cup whole wheat)
**1 cup almond or rice milk**
**¼ cup sugar**
**1 tablespoon vanilla**

In a medium saucepan over medium-high heat, melt shortening. Mix in flour with a spatula and continue stirring until small bubbles form. Whisk in almond milk until smooth. Continue to stir until mixture thickens (about 2 minutes).

Add sugar and vanilla and mix until incorporated.

Refrigerate in an airtight container for up to 1 week.

GLUTEN-FREE | 5 tbsp GLUTEN-FREE FLOUR MIX

# CHOCOLATE GANACHE
YIELD: SERVES 4

**6 tablespoons shortening**
**1¼ cups sugar**
**6 tablespoons almond or rice milk**
**1 cup vegan chocolate chips**
**1 teaspoon vanilla**

In a small saucepan over medium-high heat, mix shortening, sugar, and almond milk.

Bring to a boil for three minutes.

Remove from heat and add chocolate chips and vanilla. Mix until incorporated.

# VANILLA WAFERS

YIELD: ABOUT 150 COOKIES

½ cup shortening
¼ teaspoon pink salt
1 cup sugar
1 teaspoon vinegar
1 tablespoon vanilla
¼ cup almond or rice milk
1⅓ cups flour (1 cup + 5 tbsp whole wheat)
1¾ teaspoons baking powder

Preheat oven to 350 degrees.

Cream shortening, pink salt, and sugar.

Beat in vinegar, vanilla, and almond milk.

In a medium-sized bowl, combine flour and baking powder. Add shortening mixture and stir until incorporated.

Roll dough into teaspoon-sized balls, place onto a baking sheet, and flatten with the palm of your hand.

Bake in preheated oven for 10-15 minutes.

GLUTEN-FREE | 1⅓ CUPS GLUTEN-FREE FLOUR MIX | ¼ tsp XANTHAN GUM

# BANANA PUDDING

YIELD: SERVES 4

60 Vanilla Wafers
1½ very ripe bananas
2 cups "Custard"

Line the bottom of a 2-quart baking dish with Vanilla Wafers. Cover with "Custard" and then a layer of sliced bananas.

Repeat until all ingredients are used, ending with "Custard."

Refrigerate for at least 30 minutes before serving.

# OATMEAL RAISIN COOKIES
YIELD: 30 COOKIES

**1 cup flour** (1 cup whole wheat)
**2¾ cups rolled oats**
**1 teaspoon baking powder**
**1 teaspoon baking soda**
**¾ teaspoon cinnamon**
**½ teaspoon pink salt**
**¾ cup shortening**
**¾ cup sugar**
**¾ cup brown sugar**
**1 tablespoon apple cider vinegar**
**6 tablespoons almond milk**
**1½ tablespoons vanilla**
**1 cup raisins**

Preheat oven to 375 degrees.

In a medium-sized bowl, combine flour, oats, baking powder, baking soda, cinnamon, and pink salt.

In a large mixing bowl, cream shortening, white sugar, and brown sugar. Mix in vinegar, almond milk, and vanilla.

Add flour mixture and combine until fully incorporated. Fold in raisins.

Make ⅛ cup-sized balls of dough and place onto a baking sheet. Flatten with the palm of your hand.

Bake in preheated oven for 10-12 minutes.

Cool on a wire rack.

---

GLUTEN-FREE | 1¼ CUPS GLUTEN-FREE FLOUR MIX | ¼ tsp XANTHAN GUM

# SUGAR COOKIES
YIELD: ABOUT 24 COOKIES

**2 cups flour** (2 cups whole wheat)
**1 teaspoon baking soda**
**½ teaspoon pink salt**
**1 cup shortening**
**¾ cup sugar**
**1 tablespoon apple cider vinegar**
**1 tablespoon almond or rice milk**
**1 tablespoon vanilla**
**GLAZE**
**¼ cup shortening**
**1½ cups powdered sugar**
**1 tablespoon almond or rice milk**
**1 teaspoon vanilla**

Preheat oven to 350 degrees.

In a medium-sized bowl, combine flour, baking soda, and pink salt.

In a large mixing bowl, cream shortening and sugar until fluffy. Add vinegar, almond milk, and vanilla and mix well. Add flour mixture and combine until soft dough forms.

Divide in half.

On a lightly floured board, roll dough until ⅛-inch thick. Cut desired shapes and place onto a baking sheet.

Bake in preheated oven for 8-10 minutes.

Cool on pan for 5 minutes and then transfer to a wire rack.

MAKE GLAZE
In a medium saucepan over medium heat, melt shortening.

Remove from heat.

Whisk in powdered sugar, almond milk, and vanilla.

Cover cookies with warm glaze.

GLUTEN-FREE | 2½ CUPS GLUTEN-FREE FLOUR MIX | ¼ tsp XANTHAN GUM

# CHOCOLATE CHIP PEANUT BUTTER COOKIES
YIELD: 30 COOKIES

**1 cup flour** (1 cup whole wheat)
**1 cup rolled oats**
**1 teaspoon baking powder**
**1 teaspoon baking soda**
**½ teaspoon pink salt**
**1 cup chunky peanut butter**
**3 tablespoons shortening**
**¾ cup sugar**
**¾ cup brown sugar**
**1 tablespoon apple cider vinegar**
**5 tablespoons almond milk**
**1 teaspoon vanilla**
**1 cup vegan chocolate chips**

Preheat oven to 375 degrees.

In a medium-sized bowl, combine flour, oats, baking powder, baking soda, and pink salt.

In a large mixing bowl, cream peanut butter, shortening, white sugar, and brown sugar. Mix in vinegar, almond milk, and vanilla.

Add flour mixture and combine until fully incorporated. Fold in chocolate chips.

Make ⅛ cup-sized balls of dough and place onto a baking sheet. Flatten with the palm of your hand.

Bake in preheated oven for 10-12 minutes.

Cool on a wire rack.

GLUTEN-FREE | 1¼ CUPS GLUTEN-FREE FLOUR MIX | ¼ tsp XANTHAN GUM

# CITRUS ARROWROOT COOKIES
YIELD: ABOUT 35 COOKIES

1 cup shortening
5½ tablespoons powdered sugar
1¼ cups flour (1 cup whole wheat)
½ cup arrowroot powder
¼ teaspoon almond flavoring
¼ teaspoon orange extract
2 tablespoons almond or rice milk
CITRUS GLAZE
1 tablespoon shortening
1 cup powdered sugar
1 tablespoon lemon juice
1 tablespoon orange juice

Preheat oven to 350 degrees.

In a large mixing bowl, cream shortening, powdered sugar, flour, and arrowroot. Add almond flavoring, orange extract, and almond milk. Mix until dough forms.

Shape into tablespoon-sized balls and place onto a parchment-lined baking sheet. Flatten with the back of a spoon or the palm of your hand.

Bake in preheated oven for 10 minutes.

Cool on a wire rack and cover with citrus glaze.

CITRUS GLAZE
In a small saucepan over medium heat, melt shortening.

Whisk in powdered sugar, lemon juice, and orange juice.

GLUTEN-FREE | 1½ CUPS GLUTEN-FREE FLOUR MIX | ⅛ tsp XANTHAN GUM

# CHOCOLATE SANDWICH COOKIES
YIELD: ABOUT 60 2-INCH COOKIES

## COOKIE
1 cup cocoa powder
1¼ cups flour (1 cup whole wheat)
2 teaspoons baking powder
1 teaspoon baking soda
¼ teaspoon pink salt
1 cup shortening
2 cups sugar
¼ cup almond or rice milk
1 tablespoon apple cider vinegar
1 teaspoon vanilla
## FILLING
1 cup shortening
2¾ cups powdered sugar
⅛ cup arrowroot powder
2 tablespoons almond or rice milk
1 teaspoon vanilla

Preheat oven to 325 degrees.

MAKE COOKIES
In a medium-sized bowl, combine cocoa powder, flour, baking powder, baking soda, and pink salt.

In a large mixing bowl, cream shortening, sugar, almond milk, vinegar, and vanilla. Add cocoa mixture and stir until incorporated.

Roll on floured board until ¼-inch thick. Cut into circles and place on baking sheet.

Bake in preheated oven for 15-20 minutes. Cool on a wire rack.

MAKE FILLING
In a large mixing bowl, cream shortening, powdered sugar, arrowroot, almond milk, and vanilla.

TO ASSEMBLE
Gently spread filling over cookies and sandwich.

GLUTEN-FREE | 1½ CUPS GLUTEN-FREE FLOUR MIX | ¼ tsp XANTHAN GUM

# GANACHE BROWNIES
YIELD: 12 BROWNIES

2 cups flour (2 cups whole wheat)
2 cups sugar
¾ cup cocoa powder
1 teaspoon baking powder
½ teaspoon pink salt
1 cup warm water
1 cup grape seed oil
1 tablespoon vanilla
1 recipe Chocolate Ganache (page 186)

Preheat oven to 375 degrees.

Grease and flour a 9x13-inch baking dish.

In a large mixing bowl, combine flour, sugar, cocoa powder, baking powder, and pink salt.

Add warm water, grape seed oil, and vanilla and mix until incorporated.

Pour into the prepared baking dish and bake for 25-30 minutes (inserted toothpick should come out clean).

Cool for 15 minutes.

Cover with Chocolate Ganache.

Chill for at least 1 hour before serving.

GLUTEN-FREE | 2½ CUPS GLUTEN-FREE FLOUR MIX | ¼ tsp XANTHAN GUM

# CHOCOLATE "CREAM" CREPES
YIELD: SERVES 4

**4 Crepes** (page 59)
**1 cup "Custard"**
**½ cup Chocolate Ganache** (page 186)

Preheat oven to 350 degrees.

Wrap crepes in foil and warm in preheated oven for 10 minutes.

Spread each crepe with ¼ cup "Custard" and fold in half.

Cover each filled crepe with ⅛ cup warm Chocolate Ganache.

# STRAWBERRY CREPES
YIELD: SERVES 4

**4 Crepes** (page 59)
**2 cups sliced strawberries**
**1 cup "Custard"**

Preheat oven to 350 degrees.

Wrap crepes in foil and warm in preheated oven for 10 minutes.

Place ½ cup sliced strawberries onto each crepe and fold in half.

Cover each filled crepe with ¼ cup "Custard."

# STRAWBERRY SHORTCAKE
YIELD: SERVES 4

**2 cups chopped strawberries**
**1 tablespoon sugar**
**4 Biscuits** (page 60)
**2 cups "Custard"**

In a medium-sized bowl, combine strawberries and sugar. Let sit 5 minutes.

Cut biscuits in half. Cover each half with ¼ cup of prepared strawberries. Then with ⅛ cup "Custard."

Cover with the other biscuit half and repeat.

# TIRAMISU
YIELD: SERVES 6

## LADYFINGERS
**2 cups flour** (2 cups whole wheat)
**1 cup sugar**
**3 teaspoons baking powder**
**1 teaspoon arrowroot powder**
**¼ teaspoon pink salt**
**1 tablespoon grape seed oil**
**1 cup water**
**1 tablespoon vanilla**

**2 cups "Custard"**
**4 tablespoons nutritional yeast**
**2 cups strong organic coffee**
**cocoa powder for dusting**

MAKE LADY FINGERS
Preheat oven to 350 degrees.

Grease and flour a 9x13-inch baking dish.

In a large bowl combine flour, sugar, baking powder, arrowroot, and pink salt. Add grape seed oil, water and vanilla and mix until incorporated.

Pour batter into the prepared baking dish and bake in preheated oven for 30-35 minutes. After it's cooled completely, cut cake into ½-inch x 2-inch "fingers."

Set aside.

In a medium-sized bowl, mix "Custard" with nutritional yeast.

Soak each ladyfinger in coffee until saturated and line the bottom of a 2-quart baking dish. Cover soaked ladyfingers with 1 cup of the "Custard" mixture.

Add another layer of soaked lady fingers and then top with the remaining "Custard."

Dust with sifted cocoa powder.

Chill at least 1 hour before serving.

GLUTEN-FREE | 2¼ CUPS GLUTEN-FREE FLOUR MIX | ¼ tsp XANTHAN GUM

# LEMON BARS
YIELD: 12 BARS

## CRUST
2 cups flour (1¾ cups whole wheat flour)
¼ cup sugar
½ teaspoon pink salt
1 cup shortening

## TOPPING
3 tablespoons shortening
¼ cup flour (¼ cup whole wheat)
½ cup sugar
¾ cup almond or rice milk
5 tablespoons arrowroot powder
juice from 2 lemons
zest from 2 lemons
½ teaspoon vanilla

Preheat oven to 375 degrees.

MAKE CRUST
Mix flour, sugar, and pink salt in medium-sized bowl. Cut in shortening using your fingers. Press into the bottom of a 9x13-inch casserole dish.

Bake in preheated oven for 15 minutes.

MAKE TOPPING
In a medium saucepan over medium-high heat, melt shortening. Mix in flour with a spatula and continue stirring until small bubbles form. Whisk in almond milk until smooth. Continue to stir until mixture thickens (mixture should resemble thick paste).

Add lemon juice, sugar, and vanilla and whisk until smooth.

Pour filling over crust and refrigerate until set (about two hours).

GLUTEN-FREE | 2¾ CUPS GLUTEN-FREE FLOUR MIX | ½ tsp XANTHAN GUM
5 tbsp GLUTEN-FREE FLOUR MIX

# CARROT CAKE
YIELD: 2 10-INCH CAKES OR 24 CUPCAKES

1½ cups sugar
1 cup grape seed oil
3 teaspoons apple cider vinegar
3 tablespoons almond or rice milk
1 tablespoon vanilla
2 cups flour (2 cups whole wheat)
2 teaspoons cinnamon
3 teaspoons baking powder
1 teaspoons baking soda
3 cups shredded carrots
1 cup chopped walnuts

Preheat oven to 350 degrees.

Grease and flour 10-inch cake rounds or 24 muffin tins.

In a large mixing bowl, beat sugar, grape seed oil, vinegar, almond milk, and vanilla.

In a medium-sized bowl, combine flour, cinnamon, baking powder, and baking soda. Add to sugar mixture and mix until incorporated.

Fold in carrots and walnuts.

Pour into prepared cake pans and bake in preheated oven  for 25-30 minutes.

Cool in pan for 10 minutes. Then flip onto wire rack to cool completely.

Cover cake with "Cream Cheese" Icing.

GLUTEN-FREE  |  2¾ CUP GLUTEN-FREE FLOUR MIX  |  ¾ tsp XANTHAN GUM

# "CREAM CHEESE" ICING
YIELD: 2 CUPS

1 cup shortening
2 tablespoons nutritional yeast
¼ cup almond or rice milk
1½ teaspoons vanilla
4 cups powdered sugar

In a large mixing bowl, cream shortening, nutritional yeast, almond milk, and vanilla.

Add powdered sugar and whip until smooth.

# CHOCOLATE CAKE
YIELD: 2 10-INCH CAKES OR 24 CUPCAKES

2½ cups flour (2½ cups whole wheat)
2 cups sugar
⅔ cup cocoa powder
1 teaspoon baking powder
2 teaspoons baking soda
3 tablespoons arrowroot powder
1 teaspoon pink salt
½ cup almond or rice milk
1 cup warm water
⅔ cup grape seed oil
2 teaspoons apple cider vinegar
1 tablespoon vanilla

Preheat oven to 350 degrees.

Grease and flour 10-inch cake rounds or 24 muffin tins.

In a large mixing bowl, combine flour, sugar, cocoa powder, baking powder, baking soda, arrowroot, and pink salt.

Add almond milk, water, grape seed oil, vinegar, and vanilla. Mix until incorporated.

Pour batter into prepared pans and bake in preheated oven for 25-30 minutes.

Cool in pans for 10 minutes. Then flip onto wire rack to cool completely.

Cover cake with Chocolate "Buttercream" Icing.

GLUTEN-FREE | 2¾ CUP GLUTEN-FREE FLOUR MIX | ¾ tsp XANTHAN GUM

# CHOCOLATE "BUTTERCREAM" ICING
YIELD: 2 CUPS

1 cup shortening
¼ cup almond or rice milk
1½ teaspoons vanilla
4 cups powdered sugar
¾ cup cocoa powder

In large mixing bowl, cream shortening, almond milk, and vanilla.

Add powdered sugar and cocoa powder and whip until smooth.

# CHOCOLATE ECLAIRS
YIELD: 12 ECLAIRS

¾ cup "Custard"
¾ cup Chocolate Ganache (page 186)

**PUFF PASTRY**
¼ cup shortening
1 cup water
1 teaspoon apple cider vinegar
1¼ cups flour (1 cup whole wheat)
1 teaspoon baking powder
1 teaspoon baking soda
¼ teaspoon pink salt

MAKE PUFF PASTRY
Preheat oven to 400 degrees.

In a large saucepan over medium-high heat, melt shortening in water.

Bring to a boil.

Reduce heat to low and add vinegar.

In a medium bowl, combine flour, baking powder, baking soda, and pink salt.

Add to shortening mixture and stir vigorously until dough forms a stiff ball.

Place ⅛ cup-sized balls of dough onto a baking sheet and bake in a preheated oven for 15 minutes.

Cool on a wire rack.

Cut tops off of puff pastries and scoop out soft insides, creating a cup.

Fill each with 1 tablespoon "Custard."

Return tops and cover with 1 tablespoon Chocolate Ganache.

GLUTEN-FREE | 1¾ CUP GLUTEN-FREE FLOUR MIX | ½ tsp XANTHAN GUM

# CHERRY COBBLER
YIELD: SERVES 6

**¼ Pie Crust recipe**
**1 15 ounce can unsweetened organic cherries** (or 2 cups frozen)
**¾ cup sugar**
**3 tablespoons shortening**
**⅛ cup flour** (⅛ cup whole wheat)
**⅛ teaspoon almond flavoring**
**⅛ teaspoon vanilla flavoring**

Preheat oven to 350 degrees.

Melt 2 tablespoons shortening in a medium saucepan over medium-high heat. Mix in flour with spatula until incorporated. Keep stirring until small bubbles form. Add cherries and continue to stir until mixture thickens (about 5 minutes). Add sugar and almond flavoring.

Pour cherry mixture into a 2-quart baking dish.

Roll pie crust out until ⅛-inch thick. Cover cherries in the baking dish. Fold under excess dough and using forefinger, middle finger, and thumb, pinch around the perimeter to form a crust.

Spoon dollops of remaining shortening overtop the dough.

Bake in preheated oven until crust is golden brown (20-25 minutes).

---

GLUTEN-FREE | 3 tbsp GLUTEN-FREE FLOUR MIX

---

# MEAL PLANS
## and
# SHOPPING LISTS

# "ef-fi-cient

achieving maximum productivity with minimum wasted effort or expense."

We hope that by now you have realized that you don't have to feel like you're giving up anything to adopt a vegan diet. Even as much time and money as you may think...

It is a long founded perception that organic and vegan foods are very expensive and difficult to prepare. This isn't necessarily true. Yes, you will most likely have to devote more time to your meal preparation to use our recipes and meal plans. But we have found ways to combine meals within a week to save time, effort, and money.

Remember, we started developing our recipes for a meal delivery service and had to stay within a tight budget. We also had to cater to the tastes of a suburban area not attuned to plant-based living.

What this means for you is that no meal in this entire book costs more than $3 per person to prepare. This is less than most fast food meals. And the quality assured by your own food preparation is worth the extra effort.

And, as promised, we are going to make it easier for you. The following two weeks of meal plans, designed for a family of four, will give you a better idea of how to efficiently incorporate vegan food into your lifestyle.

After each plan, you'll see a box showing all the basic recipes needed for the week and the quantity of each to prepare. Also listed are the other recipes that should be made in bulk. This will save you time and effort.

When developing these plans, we made sure to group recipes together that included overlapping ingredients but also varied in taste and experience. Not only will this save you time, it will save money.

Each week's grocery list for four people will cost around $200- $250. Included in this grocery bounty are "pantry items." These will be used every week, but not necessarily used in full, so each week you will gradually build up your vegan pantry.

Our meal plans will keep the vegan bread on your plate and dough in your wallet!

| Meal plans should be subsidized with fresh, raw, and organic fruit. |

# WEEK 1

| | BREAKFAST | LUNCH | DINNER |
|---|---|---|---|
| **SATURDAY** | Whole Wheat Waffles | Mixed Vegetable Salads with Raw-Vegan Ranch | Enchiladas, Refried Black Beans |
| **SUNDAY** | Chocolate Chip Muffins | Grilled Vegetable and "Cheese" Sandwiches | "Cheese Burgers," Cajun Sweet Potato Fries |
| **MONDAY** | Pancakes | Vegetable Quesadillas, Refried Black Beans | Philly "Cheesesteaks," Raw-Vegan Cole Slaw |
| **TUESDAY** | Whole Wheat Waffles | Vegetable Noodle Soup, Grilled Vegetable "Cheese" Sandwiches | Brown Rice "Burger" Casserole, Side Salads with Raw-Vegan Ranch |
| **WEDNESDAY** | Berry Parfaits | Burritos, Kale Guacamole Salad | "Sausage" Kale Pizza, Side Salads with Italian Dressing |
| **THURSDAY** | Pancakes | Vegetable Noodle Soup, Mixed Vegetable Salads with Raw-Vegan Ranch | Calzones, Side Salads with Italian Dressing |
| **FRIDAY** | Chocolate Chip Muffins | Enchiladas, Side Salads with Raw- Vegan Ranch | Mushroom Kale Ravioli, Side Salad with Italian Dressing |

# WEEK 1

## RECIPE TALLY

Brown Rice (18 cups)

Pureed Eggplant (2 recipes)

Eggplant Burgers (2 recipes)

"Sausage" (1 recipe)

Soft "Cheese" (7 recipes)

Black Beans (2 recipes)

Cashew Cream (6 recipess)

Tahini (½ recipe)

Tortillas (2 recipes)

Hamburger Buns (2 recipes)

Pizza Dough (2 recipes)

Vegetable Stock (1 recipe)

Refried Black Beans (2 recipes)

Raw-Vegan Ranch (2 recipes)

Italian Dressing (2 recipes)

Enchiladas (2 recipes)

## SHOPPING LIST

### PRODUCE
4 medium eggplants
4 packages white mushrooms
6 medium red onions
2 garlic bulbs
6 heads Kale
Mixed Greens
2 bunches carrots
1 bunch celery
1 bunch parsley
4 limes
10 medium ripe avocados
2 small ripe tomatoes
3 large sweet potatoes
1 medium head green cabbage
5 medium cucumbers
2 cups green beans
2 medium green peppers
1 bunch green onions
4 medium ripe bananas
8 ounce blueberries
8 ounces strawberries

### GRAINS, NUTS, AND SEEDS
1 cup walnuts
6 cups cashews
2½ cups sesame seeds
4 ½ cups brown rice
2 cups dry Black Beans

### GROCERY
2 cans tomato paste
4 cans diced tomatoes
2 cans tomato sauce
2 tri-packs yeast
15 cups nutritional yeast
1 loaf sprouted bread
maple syrup

### FRESH HERBS
basil
oregano
thyme
dill

### PANTRY
4 quarts almond or rice milk

1 bottle coconut aminos
1 bag evaporated cane juice
brown sugar
1  5-lb bag flour
arrowroot powder
1 bottle grape seed oil
organic shortening
vegan chocolate chips
1 bottle apple cider vinegar
dijon mustard
pink salt
black pepper
marjoram
fennel
cumin
paprika
cayenne pepper
sage
bay leaves
crushed red pepper
baking powder
baking soda
vanilla flavoring

# WEEK 2

| | BREAKFAST | LUNCH | DINNER |
|---|---|---|---|
| **MONDAY** | Vegetable Quiche | Vegetable Wraps (sub Raw-Vegan Tzatziki for Raw-Vegan Ranch) | Spaghetti and "Meatballs," Side Salads with Italian Dressing |
| **TUESDAY** | Fig Breakfast Cookies | Mixed Vegetable Salads with Balsamic Vinaigrette | "Tenderloin," Scalloped Sweet Potaoes, Southern Steamed Collards |
| **WEDNESDAY** | Vegetable Quiche | "Meatball" Subs, Side Salads with Italian Dressing | Sea Vegetable Chowder, Side Salads with Balsamic Vinaigrette |
| **THURSDAY** | Fig Breakfast Cookies | "Tenderoin" Sandwiches | Mousakka, Side Salads with Raw-Vegan Tzatziki |
| **FRIDAY** | Banana Quinoa Oatmeal | Sea Vegetable Chowder, Grilled Vegatable and "Cheese" Sndwiches | Vegetable Teryiaki |
| **SATURDAY** | Sprouted Toast, Berries | Quinoa Lentil Salad, Side Salads with Raw-Vegan Tzatziki | "Cheeseburgers," Scalloped Sweet Potatoes |
| **SUNDAY** | Banana Quinoa Oatmeal | Vegetable Teryiaki | Wild Mushroom Crepes, Braised Red Cabbage, Herb Roasted Sweet Potatoes |

# WEEK 2

## RECIPE TALLY

 Brown Rice (12 cups)

 Pureed Eggplant (2 recipes)

 Eggplant "Burgers"(2 recipes)

 "Meatballs" (2 recipes)

 Soft "Cheese" (2recipes)

 Firm "Cheese" (1 recipe)

 Cashew Cream (2 recipes)

 Tahini (½ recipe)

 Tortillas (1 recipe)

 Hamburger Buns (1 recipe)

 Vegetable Stock (1 recipe)

Raw-Vegan Tzatziki (2 recipes)

Balsamic Dressing (2 recipes)

Italian Dressing (2 recipes)

Teriyaki Sauce (2 recipes)

Bechamel Sauce (2 recipes)

## SHOPPING LIST

### PRODUCE
6 medium eggplants
8 packages white mushrooms
1 cup wild mushrooms
7 medium red onions
4 garlic
5 heads Kale
mixed greens
1 bunch carrots
1 bunch celery
1 bunch parsley
1 red apple
3 lemons
9 medium sweet potatoes
1 small head red cabbage
4 medium cucumber
1 small green pepper
2 medium zucchinis
2 medium daikon roots
2 small bunches bok choy
2 inches ginger root
2 cups bean sprouts
6 ripe avocados
1 bunch green onions
8 ounces blueberries
8 ounces strawberries
½ cup dried figs

### GRAINS, NUTS, AND SEEDS
1 cups quinoa
1 cup lentils
4 1/2 cups rolled oats
¾ cup walnuts
2 cups cashews
2 ½ cups sesame seeds
3 cups brown rice

### GROCERY
1 can tomato paste
2 cans diced tomatoes
1 pkg wakame
2 tri-packs yeast
10 cups nutritional yeast
2 loaves sprouted bread
1 package brown rice spaghetti

### FRESH HERBS
basil
oregano
thyme
dill
rosemary

### PANTRY
5 quarts almond or rice milk
1 bottle coconut aminos

1 bag evaporated cane juice
1 bag brown sugar
1 5-lb bag flour
arrowroot powder
1 bottle grape seed oil
organic shortening
1 bottle balsamic vinegar
1 bottle apple cider vinegar
1 bottle dijon mustard
1 bottle ketchup
pink salt
black pepper
marjoram
fennel
baking powder
baking soda
cinnamon
cinnamon sticks
allspice
nutmeg
bay leaves
vanilla flavoring
1 bottle agave nectar

### MISC
white wine
2 vegan beers

# ENDNOTES

1 *"Quotes."* Famous Veggie, accessed March 23, 2013, http://www.famousveggie.com/quotes.aspx.

2 Joanne Stepaniak, M.S., *Being Vegan: Living with Conscience, Conviction, and Compassion.* (Los Angeles, CA: Lowell House, 2000), 1.

3 Ibid, 2.

4 Brenda Davis, R.D., Vesanto Melina, M.S, R.D. *Becoming Vegan: The Complete Guide To Adopting A Healthy Plant-Based Diet* (Summertown, TN: Book Publishing Company, 2000), 3-5.

5 Ibid, 5.

6 Stepaniak, *Being Vegan*, 2.

7 Ibid, 7.

8 Edward Howell. *Enzyme Nutrition: The Food Enzyme Concept* (Wayne, NJ: Avery Pub. Group, 1985), 2-6.

9 Ibid, 3-4

10 George Eisman, R.D. *The Most Noble Diet: Food Selection and Ethics* (Burdett, NY: Diet Ethics, 1994), 11-12.

11 "Quotes."

12 "Position of the American Dietetic Association: Vegetarian Diets." *Journal of the American Dietetic Association.* 109 (2009) 1266-1282, accessed March 12, 2013.

13 *"The Top 100 Vegan Quotes."* Pledge Vegan, accessed March 23, 2013, http://www.pledgevegan.com/vegan-spotlight/top-100-vegan-quotes.

14 Colin T. Campbell, PhD and Thomas M. Campbell II, M.D., *The China Study,* (Dallas Texas: BenBella Books, 2005), 31

15 Edmond Bordeaux Szekely, *Scientific Vegetarianism: Guide to Organic Ecological Nutrition,* (San Diego, CA: Academy Books, 1976), 41

16 Peter Singer and Jim Mason. *The Ethics of What We Eat* (Melbourne: Text Publishing, 2007), 103-105.

17 Victoria Moran, *Compassion: The Ultimate Ethic,* (Malaga, NJ: The American Vegan Society, 1991), 68

18 Ibid, 67.

19 Steve F. Sapontzis, *Food For Thought: The Debate over Eating Meat* (Amherst, NY: Prometheus Books, 2004), 49-53.

20 "The Top 100 Vegan Quotes."

21 Moran, *Compassion,* 37.

22 Joanne Stepaniak, M.S. Ed. *The Vegan Sourcebook* (Los Angeles, CA: Lowell House, 1998), 221.

23 Diane Marks, *"Dairy Products That Cause Joint Inflammation and Pain,"* Livestrong, accessed March 23, 2013, http://www.livestrong.com/article/437115-dairy-products-that-cause-joint-inflammation-pain.

24 "The Top 100 Vegan Quotes."

25 *"Vegan and Vegetarian Quotes"* Vegan Outreach, accessed March 23, 2013, http://www.veganoutreach.org/advocacy/quotes.html

26 Szekely, *Scientific Vegetarianism,* 11.

27 John Robbins, "The Ground Beneath Our Feet," in *All Heaven In a Rage,* ed. Laura A.Moretti (Chico, CA: MBK Publishing, 1994 , 127.

28 "Position of the American Dietetic Association: Vegetarian Diets."

29 Reed Mangels, PHD, RD, "Protein in the Vegan Diet."accessed March 13, 2013, http://www.vrg.org/nutrition/protein.php.

30 Campbell, *The China Study, 29-31.*

31 Mangels, :Protein in the Vegan Diet."

32 "The Top 100 Vegan Quotes."

33 *Earthlings,* DVD, dircted by Shaun Monson (2005; Nation Earth, 2005).

34 Ibid

35 "The Top 100 Vegan Quotes."

36 Eisman, *The Most Noble Diet,* 33.

37 Ibid, 33.

38 Stepamiak, *The Vegan Sourcebook,* 50.

39 "The Top 100 Vegan Quotes."

40 Stepaniak, *Being Vegan,* 35-36.

41 Singer, *The Ethics of What We Eat,* 103-105

42 *"Famous Quotes."* Easy Vegetarian, accesed March 23, 2013, http://www.easyvegetarian.net/ethicallifestyle.html

43 Stepaniak, *Being Vegan,* 34-35.

44 *"Geezer Butler."* Vegan Peace, accessed March 23, 2013, http://www.veganpeace.com/famousvegans/profiles/geezer_butler.htm.

45 Robbins, "The Ground Beneath Our Feet," (See note 27), 122.

46 Ibid, 115-119

47 Stepaniak, *The Vegan Sourcebook,* 63

48 Robbins, "The Ground Beneath Our Feet," (See note 27), 120-121.

49 "The Top 100 Vegan Quotes."

50 Robbins, "The Ground Beneath Our Feet," (See note 27), 116.

51 Ibid, 132.

52 Stepaniak, *The Vegan Sourcebook,* 64

53 Eisman, *The Most Noble Diet,* ix.

54 Robbins, "The Ground Beneath Our Feet," (See note 27), 118.

55 "The Top 100 Vegan Quotes."

56 Figono, *How Baking Works: Exporing the Fundamentals of Baking Science,* (Hoboken, NJ: John Wiley & Sons, 2011), 265-268.

57 Danielle Dellurto, "Dirty Dozen Produce Carries More Pesticide Residue, Group Says," CNN, accessed March 22, 2013, http://www.cnn.com/2010/HEALTH/06/01/dirty.dozen.produce.pesticide/index.html.

58 "Famous Quotes."

59 Lisa Weber, "The Effects of Pesticides in Foods". Livestrong, accessed March 22, 2013, http://www.livestrong.com/article/230346-the-effects-of-pesticides-in-food.

60 "Organic Produce Reduces Exposure To Pesticides, Research Confirms," Environmental Working Group. press release, September 3, 2012, on the EWG website, http://www.ewg.org/news/news-releases/2012/09/03/organic-produce-reduces-exposure-pesticides-research-confirms, accessed March 22, 2013.

61 Ibid

62 "Test Guidelines For Data Requirements." The Environmental Protection Agency, accessed June 23, 2013, http://www.epa.gov/pesticides/science/guidelines.htm.

63 "Famous Quotes."

64 ibid

65 Joseph Mercola, MD, "The Health Dangers of Soy." Huffpost Healthy Living, accessed March 23, 2013, http://www.huffingtonpost.com/dr-mercola/soy-health_b_1822466.html

66 "Famous Quotes."

67 Figono, *How Baking Works,* 309.

68 Figono, *How Baking Works,* 308.

69 "Types of Rice," Whole Grains Council, accessed March 20, 2013, http://wholegrainscouncil.org/whole-grains-101/types-of-rice.

70 Figono, How Baking Works, 330.

71 Figono, How Baking Works, 136-137.

72 "What is Celiac Disease." Celiac.com, accessed March 21, 2013, http://www.celiac.com.

73 Martha White, "Why We're Wasting Billions on Gluten-Free Food," *Time,* March 13, 2013, accessed March 23, 2013, http://business.time.com/2013/03/13/why-were-wasting-billions-on-gluten-free-food.

74 Michael Murray and Joseph Pizzorno, *The Encyclopedia of Healing Foods,* (New York: Atria Books, 2005),194-195.

74 Oxford Dictionaries. "Efficient." accessed March 24 2013, http://oxforddictionaries.com/us/definition/american_english/efficient.

# SOURCES CONSULTED

Campbell, Colin T, PhD., and Thomas M. Campbell II, M.D., *The China Study*. Dallas Texas: BenBella Books, 2005.

Celiac.com. "What is Celiac Disease." www.celiac.com. Accessed March 21, 2013. http://www.celiac.com

Daniel, Kaayla T, PhD., "The Whole Soy Story." Nutrition Digest 36(3) (2005). Accessed March 24, 2013, http://americannutritionasso-ciation.org/newsletter/whole-soy-story

Davis, Brenda, R.D. and Vesanto Melina, M.S, R.D., *Becoming Vegan: The Complete Guide To Adopting A Healthy Plant-Based Diet*. Summertown, TN: Book Publishing Company, 2000.

Delloroto, Danielle. "'Dirty Dozen Produce Carries More Pesticide Residue, Group Says." CNN.com. Accessed March 24, 2013. http://www.cnn.com/2010/HEALTH/06/01/dirty.dozen.produce.pesticide/index.html.

Earthlings. DVD. Directed by Shaun Monson. 2005; Nation Earth, 2005.

Easy Vegetarian. "Famous Quotes." Easyvegetarian.net. Accessed March 23, 2013. http://www.easyvegetarian.net/ethicallifestyle.html.

Eisman, George, R.D. *The Most Noble Diet: Food Selection and Ethics*. Burdett, NY: Diet Ethics, 1994.

Environmental Protection Agency. "Test Guidelines For Data Requirements." EPA.gov. Accessed June 23, 2013, http://www.epa.gov/pesti-cides/science/guidelines.htm.

Environmental Working Group. "Organic Produce Reduces Exposure To Pesticides, Research Confirms." Environmental Working Group. press release, September 3, 2012. Environmetal Working Group website. Accessed March 22, 2013. http://www.ewg.org/news/news-releases/2012/09/03/organic-produce-reduces-exposure-pesticides-research-confirms.

Famous Veggie "Quotes." Famousveggie.com, Accessed March 23, 2013. http://www.famousveggie.com/quotes.aspx.

Figoni, Paula. *How Baking Works: Exploring the Fundamentals of Baking Science*. Hoboken, NJ: John Wiley & Sons, 2011.

Vegan Peace. "Geezer Butler." Veganpeace.com. Accessed March 23, 2013. http://www.veganpeace.com/famousvegans/profiles/geezer_butler.htm.

Harris, William, M.D. *The Scientific Basis of Vegetarianism*. Honolulu, HI: Hawaii Health Publishers,1996.

Howell, Edward. *Enzyme Nutrition: The Food Enzyme Concept*. Wayne, NJ: Avery Publishing Group, 1985.

Kradjian, Robert M., M.D., "The Milk Letter: A Massage to My Patients." Notmilk.com. Accessed March 21, 2013. http://www.notmilk.com/kradjian.html.

Langley, Gill, M.A., PhD. *Vegan Nutrition: A Survey of Research*. Oxford: The Vegan Society Ltd, 1988.

Mangels, Reed, PhD. "Protein in the Vegan Diet." www.vrg.org. The Vegetarian Resource Group. Accessed March 13, 2013.

Mercola, Joseph, MD. "The Health Dangers of Soy." Huffpost Healthy Living. Accessed March 24, 2013. http://www.huffingtonpost.com/dr-mercola/soy-health_b_1822466.html.

Moran, Victoria. *Compassion: The Ultimate Ethic*. Malaga, NJ: The American Vegan Society, 1991.

Murray, Michael, N.D., *The Encyclopedia Of Healing Foods*. New York, NY: Atria Books, 2005.

Ory, Robert L. *Plant Proteins: Applications, Biological Effects, and Chemistry*. Washington, DC: American Chemical Society, 1986.

People For the Ethical Treatment of Animals "The Wool Industry." Accessed March 23, 2013. http://www.peta.org/issues/ani-mals-used-for-clothing/wool-industry.aspx.

Pledge Vegan, Pledge Organic. "The top 100 Vegan Quotes." Accessed March 19, 2013.

"Position of the American Dietetic Association: Vegetarian Diets." *Journal of the American Dietetic Association*. 109 (2009) 1266-1282. Accessed March 12, 2013, http://www.vrg.org/nutrition/2009_ADA_position_paper.pdf.

Robbins, John. "The Ground Beneath Our Feet." In *All Heaven in a Rage*, edited by Laura A. Moretti, 115-135. Chico, CA: MBK Publish-ing, 1994.

Sapontzis, Steve F. *Food For Thought: The Debate over Eating Meat*. Amherst, NY: Prometheus Books, 2004.

Singer, Peter and Jim Mason, *The Ethics of What We Eat*. Melbourne: Text Publishing Company, 2007.

Stepaniak, Joanne, M.S. Ed. *Being Vegan: Living with Conscience, Conviction, and Compassion*. Los Angeles, CA: Lowell House, 2000.

Stepaniak, Joanne, M.S. Ed. *The Vegan Sourcebook*. Los Angeles, CA: Lowell House, 1998.

Szekely, Edmond Bordeaux. *Scientific Vegetarianism: Guide to Organic Ecological Nutrition*. San Diego, CA: Academy Books, 1976.

Vegan Outreach . "Vegan and Vegetarian Quotes." Accessed March 23, 2013. http://www.veganoutreach.org/advocacy/quotes.html

Weber, Lisa. "The Effects of Pesticides in Foods." Livestrong. Accessed March 23, 2013. http://www.livestrong.com/article/230346-the-effects-of-pesticides-in-food.

White, Martha C. "Why We're Wasting Billions on Gluten-Free Food." *Time*, March, 13 2013. Accessed March 21, 2013. http://busi-ness.time.com/2013/03/13/why-were-wasting-billions-on-gluten-free-food.

# INDEX